Cambridge Elements ≡

Elements in Law, Economics and Politics

Series Editor in Chief
Carmine Guerriero, *University of Bologna*

Series Co-editors
Rosa Ferrer, *UPF and Barcelona GSE*
Nuno Garoupa, *George Mason University*
Mariana Mota Prado, *University of Toronto*
Murat Mungan, *George Mason University*

CAN BLOCKCHAIN SOLVE THE HOLD-UP PROBLEM IN CONTRACTS?

Richard Holden
UNSW Sydney

Anup Malani
University of Chicago

T0334081

CAMBRIDGE
UNIVERSITY PRESS

CAMBRIDGE
UNIVERSITY PRESS

University Printing House, Cambridge CB2 8BS, United Kingdom

One Liberty Plaza, 20th Floor, New York, NY 10006, USA

477 Williamstown Road, Port Melbourne, VIC 3207, Australia

314–321, 3rd Floor, Plot 3, Splendor Forum, Jasola District Centre,
New Delhi – 110025, India

103 Penang Road, #05–06/07, Visioncrest Commercial, Singapore 238467

Cambridge University Press is part of the University of Cambridge.

It furthers the University's mission by disseminating knowledge in the pursuit of education, learning, and research at the highest international levels of excellence.

www.cambridge.org
Information on this title: www.cambridge.org/9781009001397
DOI: 10.1017/9781009004794

First published 2021

A catalogue record for this publication is available from the British Library.

ISBN 978-1-009-00139-7 Paperback
ISSN 2732-4931 (online)
ISSN 2732-4923 (print)

Can Blockchain Solve the Hold-up Problem in Contracts?

Elements in Law, Economics and Politics

DOI: 10.1017/9781009004794
First published online: October 2021

The co-editors in charge of this submission were Carmine Guerriero and Rosa Ferrer.

Richard Holden
UNSW Sydney

Anup Malani
University of Chicago

Author for correspondence: Richard Holden, richard.holden@unsw.edu.au

Abstract: A vexing problem in contract law is modification. Two parties sign a contract but before they fully perform, they modify the contract. Should courts enforce the modified agreement? A private remedy is for the parties to write a contract that is robust to hold-up or that makes the facts relevant to modification verifiable. Provisions accomplishing these ends are renegotiation-design and revelation mechanisms. But implementing them requires commitment power. Conventional contract technologies to ensure commitment – liquidated damages – are disfavored by courts and themselves subject to renegotiation. Smart contracts written on blockchain ledgers offer a solution. Richard Holden and Anup Malani explain the basic economics and legal relevance of these technologies, and argue that they can implement liquidated damages without courts. They address the hurdles courts may impose to the use of smart contracts on blockchain and show that sophisticated parties' ex ante commitment to them may lead courts to allow their use as precommitment devices.

This Element also has a video abstract: www.cambridge.org/blockchain

Keywords: blockchain, commitment, hold-up, mechanism design, smart contract

ISBNs: 9781009001397 (PB), 9781009004794 (OC)
ISSNs: 2732-4931 (online), 2732-4923 (print)

Contents

1 Introduction

A fundamental problem in contract law is how to handle contract modifications (White and Summers 1988: 54; Graham and Pierce 1989: 14). Two parties sign a contract to trade some good or service. Before both sides have fully performed, the parties agree to modify the contract. Should courts enforce the modified contract?

On the one hand, the parties may have encountered a change in the environment that made the original terms suboptimal. For example, the cost of performance for the seller may have risen. Unless the price is modified, the seller would prefer to breach. Perhaps the buyer offered more of their surplus from the original contract to encourage the seller to perform in the modified contract.[1] In other words, the modified contract is the output of Coasian renegotiation that yields an efficient trade.

On the other hand, the modification may be the result of a hold-up.[2] For example, the buyer made a relationship-specific investment – that is, an expenditure that is more valuable to the parties to the contract than to non-parties to the contract.[3] In response, the seller threatens to breach unless the buyer agrees to a higher price. The buyer agrees because the loss from redeploying the investment outside the relationship is greater than the loss from paying a higher price to the seller (Corbin 1963: 105). The harm is that the hold-up discourages parties from making efficient relationship-specific investments that improve the gains from trade.[4]

Ideally, courts want to enforce modifications in the first scenario, but not the second. The central challenge of contract modification is distinguishing between these situations (Graham and Pierce 1989: 10).

One approach – which might be called a public solution – is for courts to look for evidence of changed circumstances or for modifications made under duress

---

[1] See, for example, *Watkins & Son* v. *Carrig*, 21 A.2d 591 (N.H. 1941) (upholding a modification because the contractor hired to excavate a cellar unexpectedly encountered a rock); *Angel* v. *Murray*, 322 A.2d 630 (R.I. 1974) (enforcing a modification because there was an unanticipated, substantial increase in the contractor's costs).

[2] See also Williamson (1975: 9–10, 26–28); Goldberg (1976: 439–441); and Klein et al. (1978) for non-formal discussions of the hold-up problem. See also Aghion, Dewatripont and Rey (1994: 259), presenting an early formal description of the model in the text; Holmstrom (1982: 326), presenting a more general version of the problem; and Hart and Moore (1988: 757), presenting a simpler formal description of the problem wherein only one party makes a relationship-specific investment.

[3] As a result, the party making such an investment may not recoup the full value of their investment if the relationship comes to an end and they try to market the investment to a third party.

[4] See Williamson (1975: 9–10, 26–28), describing hold-up as a form of transaction cost that reduces investment and gains from trade. More generally, see Shavell (2007: 326), noting that hold-up not only reduces investment, it can also lead to wasteful rent-seeking by the holding-up party and inefficient precautions by the potentially held-up party.

or improper threats (Posner 1977: 56; Serafine 1991; Chirelstein 1998: 65). In the former case, they enforce the modification, in the latter case they do not. The hurdle to implementing this solution is what economists call nonverifiability: parties do not have the ability to prove to courts changed circumstances or hold-up only when there in fact are changed circumstances or hold-up, respectively (Bolton and Dewatripont 2005: chs. 11–12).

To illustrate, consider the classic case of *Alaska Packers' Ass'n* v. *Domenico* (1902). Alaska Packers Association (APA) hired some fishermen in San Francisco to fish for salmon in Alaska and deliver the fish to Pyramid Harbor, Alaska, where the APA operated a cannery. The original contract paid each fisherman $50 for the season plus two cents for each salmon caught. Once the APA had sailed the fishermen to Alaska, however, the latter refused to fish unless their pay was increased to $100 for the season plus two cents for each salmon (*Domenico* v. *Alaska Packers' Ass'n* 1901: 555). Is this a case of changed circumstances or of hold-up?

The district court held for the fishermen. In its view, the APA agreed to the modification; if they were under duress, they would not have done so (*Domenico* v. *Alaska Packers' Ass'n* 1901: 555). The Ninth Circuit held for the APA. In its view, there was no consideration for the modification; so this was likely a case of duress (*Alaska Packers' Ass'n* v. *Domenico* 1902: 190). One hint at the problem of verifiability is that the two courts disagreed. Another is that Threedy's (2000) research has demonstrated that the courts did not fully understand the facts of the case. Worse, some of those facts pointed toward changed circumstances[5] and others pointed toward hold-up.[6] In short, it is likely that courts will often make mistakes about whether a modification is efficient and should be enforceable. These mistakes will likely make contracts either too inflexible or discourage relationship-specific investment, such as the APA's decision to pay to transport the fishermen to Alaska.

---

[5] First, Alaska Packers may not have been in as much duress as the Appellate Court thought, as they had leverage against the fishermen at the time of the renegotiation. For example, they could have denied them food at Pyramid Harbor (Threedy 2000: 217). Alaska Packers also had insurance against renegotiation. Alaska Packers Association was part of an association of canneries that insured each other against losses at any specific cannery, including the one at Pyramid Harbor. Moreover, the cannery at Pyramid Harbor was a small component of Alaska Packers' total production and that cannery had other suppliers of fish – for example, local Native American tribes (Threedy 2000: 200, 212, 215–216). Second, some facts suggest that the fishermen's costs were higher than they expected. The fishermen were taught that nets were not to be reused season to season. Alaska Packers, however, had bought a new type of net that allowed reuse. It is possible the fishermen reasonably thought that the nets were inadequate (Threedy 2000: 205–208).

[6] The fishermen seemed to have signed a low-price contract but only realized it when they arrived at Pyramid Harbor and met other fishermen making double their wage (Threedy 2000: 205–208). In addition, many of the facts suggesting that Alaska Packers may not have been in duress or that the fishermen's costs had risen may not actually establish that.

An alternative approach – which might be called a private solution – is for the parties to write better contracts. One example is a contract that is completely state-contingent: it anticipates and prescribes terms of trade under all possible changed circumstances (Bolton and Dewatripont 2005: ch. 11). The challenge with this approach is that complete contracts are costly to write and courts may not be able to enforce them because, again, the changed circumstances are not verifiable to courts (Bolton and Dewatripont 2005: ch. 11).

Another example of a better contract is one that includes contract provisions that either encourage relationship-specific investment even in the presence of hold-up[7] or incentivizes parties not to lie about changed circumstances.[8] Economists call the former provisions a "renegotiation design mechanism" and the latter provisions a "revelation mechanism." The challenge with these mechanisms is that they require that the parties are able to commit to the rules prescribed by those mechanisms (Holden and Malani 2014: 157–160). If either party refused to comply with those rules, the mechanisms would fail.

There are conventional contractual tools that parties could employ to provide commitment. For example, parties can include liquidated damages clauses if either party fails to follow the rules set forth under one or the other mechanism. Unfortunately, parties often have an incentive to renegotiate liquidated damages clauses after they are triggered, so they are never enforced. Other times, courts do not enforce liquidated damages clauses that are in excess of the economic damages, so-called penalty clauses, even though it is exactly such clauses that best encourage compliance.

Recently two new technologies have emerged – blockchain and smart contracts – that might make it easier for parties to commit to renegotiation design and revelation mechanisms. One contribution of our Element is to explain the economic and legal relevance of these two technologies.

Blockchain is a computer science innovation that enables the creation of distributed, open and unalterable ledgers. What that means is that a transaction on a computer network with blockchain infrastructure, also called a blockchain network, is witnessed by others on the network (decentralized), is made public to everyone on the network (open) and cannot be changed without a tremendous amount of computing power or cost (unalterable).

---

[7] See Aghion, Dewatripont and Rey (1994: 263–265), suggesting the use of default trade terms and take-it-or-leave-it offers to structure renegotiation; and Noldeke and Schmidt (1995: 168–171), suggesting the use of options to restructure renegotiation.

[8] See Maskin (1977), suggesting a simple revelation mechanism that admits a truthful Nash equilibrium; and Moore and Repullo (1988: 1208, 1212), suggesting a more complicated mechanism but that rules out non-truthful equilibria.

Smart contracts are computer scripts that execute transactions, including transactions that constitute mutual promises between contracting parties, now and in the future. When created on blockchain, the future transactions envisioned in the smart contract are automatically executed and, because of the inalterability of blockchain, cannot practically be stopped.

Our central claim is that, by virtue of these features, smart contracts on blockchain are able to impose liquidated damages that cannot be renegotiated, or enjoined or reversed by courts. As such, they allow parties to more credibly and robustly commit to contracts, including renegotiation design mechanisms that protect investments against hold-up or revelation mechanisms that help courts verify changed circumstances.

Smart contracts on blockchain are not guaranteed to work, but we think they are a significant improvement over the status quo contracting technologies. The biggest obstacle to blockchain solutions is the government. It is possible courts or Congress would ban smart contracts and/or blockchain. But we believe blockchain has enough value, especially to the financial services sector, that collateral costs will deter the government from banning our solution. The government could ban specific uses of smart contracts and blockchain, for example, stopping automation of future promises or certain contract penalty provisions. But this is unlikely as both parties to a contract want these terms ex ante. It is only ex post that one party does not prefer them. As with liquidated damages, we think the risk of court intervention is mainly limited to cases of bargaining-power imbalance.

It is also possible that even sophisticated parties may simply make a mistake in the economic design or technical details of the smart contract, or fail to fully anticipate future states of nature. In such instances, it could be that there is a pareto improvement to the initial contract and, as such, both parties would like to renegotiate the contract ex post. The degree to which these circumstances are likely depends on the primitives of the economic environment.

Finally, our solution cannot overcome the so-called common knowledge problem that limits the power of renegotiation mechanisms to prevent hold-up. To be sure, neither can existing contracting techniques. However, blockchain, by making all transactions open, may be able to reduce the severity of the common knowledge problem to some extent.

In addition to the literatures on property-rights theory, the hold-up problem and revelation mechanisms, we clearly also connect to a burgeoning literature on blockchain. Of particular relevance are recent contributions by Arruñada and Garicano (2018), Budish (2018), Tinn (2017), Siegfried, Rosenthal and Benlian (2020), Saleh (2021) and Zheng et al. (2018).

Arruñada and Garicano (2018) make the important observation that blockchain, as a decentralized solution that allows members of a network to "split," can help reduce hold-up but also hinders coordination among members of the network. They analyze this important tradeoff theoretically, and provide evidence of centralized governance in networks with significant relational capital such as Apple and Google.

Budish (2018), in an elegant paper, demonstrates that blockchain technologies relying on "Proof of Work" are on a kind of collision-course with themselves. In particular, his framework establishes the fact that a currency such as Bitcoin "would be majority attacked if it became sufficiently economically important." Thus, there is an inherent limit to the degree to which a digital currency such as Bitcoin, in its current form, can act as a store of value.

Siegfried, Rosenthal and Benlian (2020) explore how blockchain relates to, and can be an important feature of, the "Internet of Things." Christidis and Devetsikiotis (2016) also connect "Proof of Stake" to such applications.

Saleh (2021) and Zheng et al. (2018) all analyze "Proof of Stake" as an alternative consensus protocol to "Proof of Work." It is well known that "Proof of Work" involves large electricity consumption (Bitcoin being the most famous example), making "Proof of Stake" a potentially important alternative. Of particular interest, Saleh (2021) offers conditions under which "Proof of Stake" indeed generates consensus in the sense that there exists an equilibrium in which consensus is reached maximally quickly and also does not admit an equilibrium in which a fork persists.

Section 2 provides examples of hold-up problems from case law and explains the economics of the hold-up problem, demonstrates how renegotiation design and revelation mechanisms work, and discusses the information hurdles to implementing these mechanisms to tackle the contract modification problem. Section 3 explores how courts have attempted to tackle the problem of contract modification and pre-blockchain private remedies that may reduce the hold-up problem, as well as the limits of both of these tactics. Section 4 summarizes the general economic innovation from and legal relevance of blockchain and smart contracts. Section 5 shows how smart contracts on blockchain can help reduce hold-up or verify changed circumstances better than existing doctrinal or contractual approaches. The section also examines some of the limitations of smart contracts on blockchain. The conclusion makes predictions about the implications of our argument for the size of firms and output. It also speculates about the benefits of smart contracts and blockchain for contract law more generally.

2 The Hold-up Problem, Its Impact and Mechanism Design

The hold-up problem is what makes the enforceability of contract modification a difficult question for courts. Without hold-up, modifications would simply reflect changed circumstances and efficient renegotiation. Courts could simply enforce all modifications. With the possibility of hold-up, modifications may be inefficient. As a result, it is critical that courts or the parties be able to rule out or minimize the impact of modifications that are the result of hold-up. Given the centrality of hold-up to the challenge of contract modification, this section elaborates on its prevalence, its impact and contractual mechanisms designed to address it.

2.1 The Hold-up Problem and Its Impacts

In order to illustrate the costs of the hold-up problem and, later, its possible theoretical solutions, we use a recent example that should be familiar to readers, at least those familiar with smart phones. The buyer in our example is Apple, an original equipment manufacturer ("OEM") of the iPhone smartphone, and the seller is Corning, an important component manufacturer that produces "Gorilla Glass." Our contention is not that Apple and Corning's contract actually had a hold-up problem but that it might have and that we can therefore use it to illustrate some of the impacts of hold-up and solutions to hold-up. The numbers we employ in this example were chosen not because they reflect reality but because they help demonstrate how hold-up can deter efficient investment.[9]

Suppose Apple and Corning want to enter into a relationship wherein Corning provides 1 unit of a good ("Gorilla Glass" or "glass") at price, p, per unit.[10] The value generated by the trade depends on Apple's valuation for the glass, v, and Corning's cost of producing the glass, c.

The timing of the relationship is as follows. First, the parties contract. Second, they make their investments noncooperatively and simultaneously. Third, they both learn v and c. Finally, the contract is executed.

---

[9] As Shavell (2007: 330) has noted, this is not the only cost of hold-up, though the other costs are derivative of this one. Potential victims, to avoid the costs of hold-up, may take great efforts to avoid hold-up, including using multiple suppliers even though one is sufficient or lining up alternative suppliers before they are required. Conversely, potential perpetrators of hold-up may engage in inefficient activities to engineer duress, for example, using more expensive manufacturing or service methods than required so as to credibly claim higher costs.

[10] Instead of dealing with quantities traded, our example will deal with the probability of trade. However, our example does not depend on the buyer only obtaining 1 unit of the good in question because we can define a unit as a lot of any arbitrary number of submits, for example, crates of 1,000 individual glass plates. In this context, a purchase of 500 glass plates can be described as a half probability of buying 1 crate of glass plates.

At the time of contracting, the precise values of v and c are not known since they depend on investments made by Apple and Corning. We propose some numbers that have no special significance but can help the reader see how the hold-up problem operates. Suppose that v can be either $40 or $32 and correspondingly c can be $16 or $10.[11] Apple's investment affects the probability that v is high (or low) and Corning's investment affects the probability that c is high (or low). These investments are privately costly to Apple and Corning, costing each $5. One can think of Apple's investment as marketing of the iPhone, thus increasing sales volume, or as Apple making other features of the iPhone more complementary with strong glass – say by having a smaller form-factor, reduced bezel or adding a face recognition system that eliminates the need for a thumbprint ID-enabled home button and allows the screen to take up the entire front of the smartphone. One can think of Corning's investment as improving the strength of the glass, especially larger pieces of glass, or lowering the cost of production.

The parties do not write fully state-contingent contracts that specify p and the probability of trade q for each combination of v and c and they only invest after they contract because, in reality, there are unanticipated innovations, opportunities or challenges that arise after contracting but before delivery. Real-world examples include Samsung's surprise introduction of a glass screen that folds around the edges of their Galaxy phone (see, e.g., Samsung Galaxy 6). Corning felt pressure to match that. Another real-world example is Apple's surprise filing of a facial recognition system that increases the value of a larger glass plate front from Corning (Crook 2017). Apple would not want to announce the patent earlier for fear that competitors or even suppliers might file their related patents earlier.

With the numbers we have chosen in our example, the socially efficient thing to do is for both parties to make the investments, since both have a marginal value above their marginal cost ($8 compared to $5 for Apple's investment and $6 compared to $5 for Corning's). If the investments are made, then the total surplus is $40 − $10 − $5 − $5 = $20.

The essence of the hold-up problem, however, is that Apple and Corning will underinvest in the absence of the ability to contract on the investments (or values/costs) if they cannot prevent renegotiation. To see this, consider Corning, and suppose that they make their privately costly investment. Once Apple's value for the glass and Corning's cost of producing it is realized, the parties will renegotiate the price, since contracting was incomplete at the start of the

---

[11] The numbers in this example borrow heavily from a numerical example in Holden and Malani (2014: 164–169).

relationship. Assuming, for simplicity, that the parties evenly split the incremental surplus generated (as would arise as a result of the Nash bargaining solution), then the price will be adjusted so that Corning only gets half of the $6 that it increased total surplus by, that is $3. Anticipating this at the investment stage, Corning compares the $3 benefit with the $5 cost and will not invest. Analogously, Apple will compare a $8/2 = $4 benefit with a $5 cost and likewise will not invest. This means that, in the presence of hold-up, neither party will invest, Apple's valuation will be low and Corning's cost high, and total surplus will be $32 − $16 = $16.

As our numerical example illustrates, hold-up reduces economic surplus. It is thus natural, therefore, that economists have spent considerable effort[12] exploring how its impact can be mitigated, in circumstances where it cannot be avoided due to limitations of the contracting environment.

2.2 Using Renegotiation-Design Mechanisms to Address Hold-up

The difficulties with hold-up derive from the subsequent renegotiation of prices. Economists have designed a number of contracting solutions – called "mechanisms" – to tackle the hold-up problem. The logic behind these mechanisms stem from the observation that if this renegotiation could be structured differently, then perhaps the social optimum could be obtained despite hold-up. Chung (1991) and Aghion, Dewatripont and Rey (1994) are leading examples of this approach. We illustrate how renegotiation design mechanisms work using the mechanism in Aghion, Dewatripont and Rey (1994), henceforth "ADR." In Appendix A, we illustrate another important renegotiation mechanism based on options contracts, attributable to Noldeke and Schmidt (1995).

The ADR mechanism has two components. The first component is a default trade that can always be requested by one party, even if it is held-up. This default option is structured to give that party (say the seller) a full return to its investment for sure. This needs to be enforceable with a specific performance remedy or a liquidated damages remedy that strongly incentivizes specific performance if the party with the default option requests the default trade. The second component gives all the bargaining power in renegotiation to the other party (say the buyer), by allowing that party to make a take-it-or-leave-it offer. The timing of the renegotiation game is as follows: (1) the parties make

---

[12] This is reflected in a number of Nobel Prizes related to this literature. After Ronald Coase won the prize for his transaction cost theory of firm size, Oliver Williamson won it in 2009 in large part for his work on hold-up. Jean Tirole won in 2014 for a range of contributions, one of which was his work on renegotiation design mechanisms. Finally, Oliver Hart won the prize in 2016 for explaining how asset ownership and residual rights of control can promote efficient ex ante investment and thus provide a theory of vertical and lateral integration.

investment decisions; (2) the buyer makes a take-it-or-leave-it offer; and (3) the seller can accept the offer (in which case trade takes place on those terms) or can trigger the default trade. This two-stage mechanism achieves the socially optimal level of investment by both parties. To see why, note that the seller, despite having no bargaining power at the take-it-or-leave-it stage, is the residual claimant on their investment due to their access to the default option in the second stage of the game, and thus has appropriate incentives to invest optimally. Inducting back to the take-it-or-leave-it-stage, the buyer, because it has all the bargaining power, has the requisite incentives to invest optimally (Aghion, Dewatripont and Rey 1994: 263–266).

To see how this renegotiation game plays out in the Apple–Corning example,[13] there is a single unit of glass to be traded, so it is convenient to think of setting the default probability that a widget will be traded. The first component of the ADR mechanism is the default trade that Corning can trigger. We set the default probability of trade at 5/6 and the default price at $23 1/3. We will not go through a derivation of the numbers we have chosen here,[14] but they are constructed to do two things: split the ex ante surplus evenly between Apple and Corning, and ensure that Corning has the appropriate incentives to make the cost-reducing investment. The second component of the ADR mechanism is to give Apple the right to make a take-it-or-leave-it offer.

What is the best offer for Apple to make when they get the opportunity? Since Apple is making a take-it-or-leave-it offer, they have all the bargaining power and will thus want to trade the efficient amount of glass, which is 1 unit. Apple, possessing all the bargaining power, will extract Corning's entire surplus. This leaves Corning indifferent between the default option and accepting Apple's offer. Corning will thus anticipate getting the same payoff as under the default option, whatever happens.

Now work backward, and consider Corning's decision whether to invest at the earlier stage. If Corning invests, they get a payoff equal to $23 1/3 − (5/6) × $10 − $5 = $10 (the price minus probability of trade multiplied by the cost of production, minus the investment cost). If Corning does not invest, they get a payoff equal to $23 1/3 − (5/6) × $16 = $10. So, Corning is willing to invest.[15]

---

[13] This description is based heavily on Holden and Malani (2014: 162–164).

[14] A general derivation is as follows. Suppose that the valuation, v, to the buyer is either v_L or v_H and the seller's cost of production is either c_L or c_H. Trade takes place at price, p. The buyer can invest j at cost $\phi(j)$, which makes the probability of the high valuation equal to j. Similarly, the seller can invest amount i at cost $\phi(i)$, which leads to the probability of the low-cost state being i. The buyer's payoff is thus $vq − p − \phi(j)$, and the seller's is $p − cq − \phi(i)$. Let the default option be a price quantity pair $(\widetilde{p}, \widetilde{q})$. Set the default level of trade such that $\widetilde{q}(c_H − c_L) = \phi'(i^{FB})$, where ^{FB} denotes the first-best level of investment. The default price is set to split the surplus according to the respective bargaining weights of the two parties.

[15] It is easy to break the indifference slightly in favor of investing without altering the analysis.

Now consider Apple, who is the residual claimant on their investment. They obtain $8 if they make the investment, but bear a cost of just $5. So, Apple also makes the efficient investment. Thus, total surplus is $40 − $10 − $5 − $5 = $20. Remarkably, this is the first best − the same as if Apple and Corning could contract on all relevant contingencies.

It is, at first glance, rather surprising that Corning finds it optimal to invest despite having none of the bargaining power in the renegotiation. The key is their ability to reject Apple's offer and trigger trade under the terms of the default option. The default option becomes more appealing when the glass is low cost, which happens precisely when Corning invests. In other words, the presence of the default option makes Corning's payoff sensitive to their investment.

Of course, there are also legal doctrines that alter the ex post bargaining power of each party. Notable examples of this are highlighted in Guerriero (2020) and Guerriero and Pignataro (2021). In our preceding example, this might involve increasing Corning's bargaining power by strengthening remedies for "unfair contract terms," "abuse of right" and "compulsory licensing." And Apple's bargaining power is affected by "non-disclosure," "work for hire" and "non-compete" agreements. When the investments by the two parties are sufficiently complementary, this can play an important role.[16]

2.3 Mechanisms to Address Nonverifiability More Generally

So far, we have examined the problem of hold-up when the parties make relationship-specific investments, like Alaska Packers' chartering of a ship to take plaintiff fishermen to Alaska, or in our Apple and Corning example. However, there may be important ex post inefficiencies that arise from the inability to write complete, state-contingent contracts even in the absence of relationship-specific investments.

The economics literature has only recently made progress in providing formal models of such ex post inefficiencies, typically through the use of ingredients from social psychology such as "reference points" (see Hart and Moore 2008). We will not delve into those formal models here. However, we do highlight solutions to these ex post inefficiencies that do not restructure renegotiation so much as to get the parties to truthfully report nonverifiable information to the court, making that information verifiable.

Beginning with Maskin (1977), a large literature has explored how carefully crafted mechanisms that require players to make announcements, and face payoffs dependent on those announcements, may be able to cause information

---

[16] We thank an anonymous referee for pointing this out to us.

observable to players but not to outsiders to *become* observable and thus verifiable by outsiders. This is particularly useful in the hold-up setting, because once the parties know that the true state will be revealed, then they can ex ante contract on v or c, even if they cannot contract on relationship-specific investments per se.[17]

An illustration of Maskin's theorem in the Apple–Corning setting is as follows. To make Apple's value v – which both Apple and Corning know once it is realized – verifiable to a court, each party is asked to simultaneously announce 40 or 32. The mechanism specifies that if both parties agree in their announcement, then that is the stipulated value of v. If the parties disagree, then each pays a very large fine to a third party.

It is straightforward to see that both Apple and Corning announcing truthfully is a Nash equilibrium. Suppose v is actually 40. Conditional on Apple announcing "40," the Corning's best response is to announce "40" as they avoid the large fine. Unfortunately, both parties not announcing truthfully is also a Nash equilibrium. Suppose again that v is actually 40, conditional on Apple announcing "32," the best response of Corning is to announce "32" to avoid the fine.

Troubled by this multiplicity of equilibrium, Moore and Repullo (1988: 1208, 1212) show that by using a multi-stage mechanism, set forth in Appendix B, it is possible to implement any social objective as the unique (subgame–perfect) equilibrium of the game induced by that mechanism.

2.4 Information Problems That Hamper Mechanisms

Rarely, if ever, are the renegotiation design or the revelation mechanisms described seen in practice (Shavell 2007: 347–348). This begs the question: Why not? One reason may be that these mechanisms seem too complex to implement as they require two or three stages of structured bargaining. Holden and Malani (2014: 155) show that these hurdles cannot be too large because, while uncommon, procedures like the ADR mechanism can be found in, for example, variable quantity contracts. Moreover, even the multi-stage procedures in Moore–Repullo mechanisms are less complicated than some arbitration procedures to which contractual parties agree, let alone actual trials and the civil procedure rules that govern contracts in the absence of arbitration provisions.

2.4.1 Uncertainty

Another explanation for why the aforementioned mechanisms are uncommon is the substantial information requirements of these mechanisms. One piece of

---

[17] For example, they can limit how much p rises when v is high or p falls when c is low so as to ensure each party has adequate incentives to invest in raising v or lowering c.

information required is that the parties need to know the cost and payoffs to each type of investment to employ these mechanisms. For example, both parties must know the cost of the Corning's investment ($5) and the amount that it will reduce costs c (from $16 to $10) in order to set the default option (trade of 5/6 a unit for $23 1/3). Often these numbers are uncertain. In that case, the parties cannot precisely structure the mechanism, which in turn means that the mechanism may not always deter hold-up.

If this sort of uncertainty looms large, the parties can only avoid renegotiation by foregoing renegotiation of their original contract altogether. We will discuss how this might be achieved without and with blockchain in Sections 3 and 5, respectively. The downside of this approach is that parties lack the flexibility to renegotiate when there is no hold-up but there are changed circumstances such that both parties would benefit from a different bargain than the original contract.

2.4.2 Information Asymmetry

A different sort of problem arises if there is information asymmetry between the parties. Aghion et al. (2012) argue, theoretically, that complex mechanisms are not robust to small perturbations from common knowledge. We will not go into the intricate details of their logic here, but their claim hinges on the observation that these mechanisms implicitly assume not just that the state of nature is observable to the contracting parties but that it is also *common knowledge* among the contracting parties. In other words, the mechanisms assume that Apple and Corning not only observe v and c but agree on what v and c are.[18]

Aghion et al. (2012) then show that these mechanisms are not robust to an arbitrarily small perturbation away from common knowledge – that is, to Apple and Corning honestly disagreeing even slightly about the value of v or c. In this context, two-stage renegotiation-design mechanisms like ADR may yield optimal trade and thus investment, but they may also yield equilibria with suboptimal trade and investment. In other words, investment is not the unique equilibrium of those mechanisms (Aghion et al. 2012: 1870, 1875).

Things get worse with more complicated, three-stage mechanisms such as that of Moore and Repullo (Aghion et al. 2012: 1863). With those, arbitrarily small deviations from common knowledge causes not just the emergence of non–truth-telling as an equilibrium, it causes truth-telling to no longer be an

---

[18] It may seem strange that both Apple and Corning can observe v and c but not see the same thing. The reason may be that both get some information on v and c that is unbiased but not precise – that is, they see v and c plus some random noise. In that context, the two parties get equal quality information on v and c but do not agree on v or c.

equilibrium. In other words, the parties cannot even contract on v and c because they will never be truthfully revealed.[19]

Experimental evidence from Aghion et al. (2017) supports this theoretical finding with respect to revelation mechanisms in particular, but also offers some hope. They show that revelation mechanisms underperform due to asymmetric information, but that the degree of underperformance is proportional to the degree of asymmetric information (Aghion et al. 2017: 27). In other words, the lesser the information asymmetry, the better the performance of revelation mechanisms, even though they do not achieve perfect truthfulness and thus maximal investment incentives.

3 Possible Solutions to the Hold-up Problem

There are a number of ways that parties and courts can, in practice, address the problem of hold-up, though each approach has its shortcomings. We will first discuss what role courts can play, in order to review doctrinal responses to the risk of hold-up during contract modifications. Nearly all either fail to allow efficient modifications or permit hold-up, or require knowledge of facts that may not be verifiable to a court. We will then discuss private solutions that can be employed without smart contracts on blockchain and their limitations.

3.1 Public Solutions

Historically, courts took a dim view of modifications. They applied the preexisting duty rule, which stated that doing what a party had already promised to do is insufficient consideration for a new promise.[20] This is formally the rule that the Ninth Circuit applied to invalidate the modification in *Alaska Packers' Ass'n* v. *Domenico* (1902: 102), though as we will see, it has nonetheless come to be interpreted as standing for a different rule.[21]

The problem with the preexisting duty rule is that it made it difficult to implement contract modifications that were efficient responses to changed circumstances (Graham and Pierce 1989: 14). It was also easily gamed with

---

[19] The reason for the more dismal result with three-stage mechanisms is that the party that plays in the second stage not only has no incentive to tell the truth but has an incentive to lie because the other party gets to play again after them. With two-stage mechanisms, player 2 does not have to worry about what player 1 will do after they move.

[20] See, for example, *Rose* v. *Daniels*, 8 R.I. 381 (1866) (holding that a modification to a loan agreement that discharged the debt for a sum lower than the amount due was unenforceable because it was not supported by consideration). See also, Vol. 1A Corbin (1963: § 171, 105) ("[N]either the performance of duty nor the promise to render performance already required by duty is sufficient consideration for a return promise.").

[21] It has been argued that the justification for the preexisting duty or no-consideration rule is really duress (Posner 1977: 56; Graham and Pierce 1989: 13; Serafine 1991).

small amounts of consideration, which largely preserved the rents earned by exploitative contracting parties (Murray 1974: 179; Calamari and Perillo 1983: § 4–9, at 207; Graham and Pierce 1989: 14). As a result, the rule has largely been abandoned (Graham and Pierce 1989: 14–15).

In its stead, courts have largely followed three different rules. The first and most widespread in common law is the duress doctrine, under which courts may rule a modification unenforceable if they determine it was secured under duress. Duress is typically defined as induced by an "improper threat," including a threat of breach (see, e.g., *Hartsville Oil Mill* v. *United States* 1926; *Sistrom* v. *Anderson* 1942; *Steinberg Press, Inc.* v. *Charles Henry Publications, Inc.* 1947; Jolls 1997: 207), especially if the threat leaves the victim with "no reasonable alternatives" (Restatement (Second) of Contracts 1979: §§ 175(1), 176(1)(d)). The definition of duress has expanded over time and has been criticized for being ambiguous (Graham and Pierce 1989: 10).

The second rule is good faith. The comment to Uniform Commercial Code § 2–209, which governs modification to contracts for the sale of goods only, explains that "modifications . . . must meet the test of good faith." However, this requirement largely overlaps with the duress test; the comment explains that "the extortion of a 'modification' without legitimate commercial reason is ineffective as a violation of the duty of good faith."

The third rule is the "changed circumstances" rule. Under this rule, courts look for unanticipated changes in commercial conditions that would make the original contract unappealing for the parties (*Angel* v. *Murray* 1974). If found, the court would enforce a modification. In contrast with the duress doctrine, in which courts look for evidence (duress) that a modification is bad, with the changed circumstances rule, courts look for evidence that a modification is good.

The Restatement (Second) of Contracts effectively endorses all three rules at once. While the background rule is that contracts (or contract modifications) lacking consideration are unenforceable (Restatement (Second) of Contracts 1979: § 73), the Restatement carves an exception: modifications unsupported by consideration are still enforceable if they are "fair and equitable in view of circumstances not anticipated by the parties when the contract was made" (Restatement (Second) of Contracts 1979: § 89). However, a modification is not enforceable if it is induced by an "improper threat," which includes a threat to breach in violation of the duty of good faith (Restatement (Second) of Contracts 1979: §§ 175(1), 176(1)(d)).

Scholars have proposed alternative rules, although these have not gained traction in case law. For example, Shavell (2007: 326) has advocated a rule that allows modifications, so long as the change in price is reasonable. Bar Gill and

Ben Shahar (2004: 392) have proposed a rule that would allow modifications even if induced by threats so long as those threats are credible. Jolls (1997: 204) has gone so far as to suggest that courts allow the parties to contract to disallow any future modifications to a contract.[22]

The different rules enforced by courts, as well as alternative rules proposed by scholars, all suffer from a basic problem: non-verifiability. For example, the duress doctrine depends on demonstrating improper threat and the lack of alternatives. Likewise, Bar Gill and Ben Shahar's proposal requires distinguishing between credible and non-credible threats. The changed circumstances rule requires proof of unanticipated alteration in economic conditions surrounding the contract. There may be disagreements about whether there was an improper or credible threat or an increase in costs, as exemplified by Threedy's (2000) exegesis of the facts behind *Alaska Packers' Ass'n* v. *Domenico* (1901).

What makes matters more complicated is that the existence of, say, changed circumstances is not sufficient evidence that a modification should be enforced from an economic perspective. What the court should do, as Shavell explains, is compare the increase in costs due to changed circumstances with the increase in price. If the increase in price is greater than the increase in costs, then there may be hold-up even in the presence of changed circumstances. Yet, these careful economic calculations are not the comparative advantage of courts.[23]

Even if ex post courts can overcome these disagreements about facts and reach a decision, ex ante there will be uncertainty among the parties about what rule the courts will apply or which facts the court will find. This uncertainty implies that there is a positive probability that remedies will be inadequate.[24] That in turn creates opportunities for hold-up.

Some rules, such as the preexisting duty rule and Joll's rule to enforce no-modifications clauses, are easy for courts to enforce and entail little uncertainty.

---

[22] Courts presently do not allow such provisions. Restatement (Second) of Contracts (1979: § 311 cmt. a); see also *Beatty* v. *Guggenheim Exploration Co.*, 122 N.E. 378, 387 (N.Y. 1919); *Davis* v. *Payne & Day, Inc.*, 348 P.2d 337, 339 (Utah 1960); *Zumwinkel* v. *Leggett*, 345 S.W.2d 89, 93–94 (Mo. 1961). A problem with this solution is that it is extreme: it rules out efficient modifications in response to changed circumstances. This could be optimal if there was no way to distinguish such efficient modifications from inefficient modifications due to hold-up. We are not ready to do that, as the mechanisms described in sections II.C and II.D of the Restatement, if they could be implemented, would allow private parties to do better than pre-committing to no modification ever.

[23] The lack of comparative advantage in making economic judgments is why, in corporate law for example, courts apply a business judgment rule that asks whether directors have followed a careful process before taking important corporate decisions rather than examining the economic merits of the corporate decision itself (Easterbrook 1987: 894).

[24] Because courts do not adjust damages upward to reflect the probability that they would come to a different (or wrong) conclusion about liability, it is necessarily the case that expected damages are inadequate (Polinsky and Shavell 1998: 887).

Yet, these are also extreme solutions. Each rules out any efficient modifications in response to changed circumstances.

3.2 Private Solutions

Given the inherently limited ability of courts to tackle the problem of hold-up, at least without going overboard and stopping even efficient modifications, we turn to private, contractual solutions that parties may pursue – with less reliance on nuanced judgment by courts – to address the risk or consequences of hold-up.

Ideally, the parties would write a contract that precisely specified the investments each party would make in each state of the world and at the price and quantity that they would trade given the result of those investments. Economists call this a complete state-contingent contract that specifies the parties' payoffs in all states of the world. In this context, courts would have no reason to allow renegotiation – correctly or mistakenly – because the original contract would account for all possible changed circumstances. That, in turn, would deter hold-up.

Yet, such contracts are nearly impossible to write. Parties may not know all possible states or it may not be cost effective to specify them all ex ante. Moreover, courts often cannot verify what state the parties are in and thus enforce the appropriate contractual provision. Indeed, this is the reason that the starting assumption of the economic literature on the hold-up problem is that parties cannot and do not write, or courts cannot enforce, complete contracts (Hart and Moore 1990: 1126; Aghion and Holden 2011: 182).

One alternative solution is for the two contracting parties to merge and conduct the transaction internally within a single firm. This option is why Coase and later Grossman and Hart (and Hart and Moore) suggested that hold-up could provide incentives for the parties to move their transaction from the market, mediated by contract between firms, to organizing the transaction within a single, integrated firm.

While Apple and Corning integrating would address the glass plate supply problem, both parties also deal with other suppliers and purchasers. Corning cannot both integrate with Apple and with, say, Motorola, another smartphone OEM. As a result, integrating with Apple would mean having a less efficient relationship with Motorola, due to hold-up. Nor would Apple want to own every single one of its thousands of suppliers, even though their deals may also entail hold-up risks. Managing all of those relationships internally within a firm simply replaces hold-up problems with internal agency problems.

A second alternative for the parties is to rely on repeat play and reputation. If Apple and Corning transact each year for each new iteration of Apple's smartphone, they each have a strong incentive not to hold the other up, lest they jeopardize future deals between them (Klein et al. 1978: 302, explaining the value of long-term contracts). That said, if the power to hold-up is asymmetric, it would affect the aggregate division of gains from trade across all the parties' contracts in favor of the party with more hold-up power. This in turn could reduce the incentive of the weaker party to participate even in repeat play transactions. More importantly, many parties do not transact repeatedly – or expect that their repeated transactions will one day end.[25] In that context, parties must rely on market reputation. The challenge is that, if courts cannot verify hold-up, other companies might not be able to either.

A third alternative is for the parties to employ one of the renegotiation design or revelation mechanisms discussed in Section 2. For instance, they could specify default trades that favor one party and give the other party the right to make a take-it-or-leave-it offer, as the ADR mechanisms suggest (Aghion, Dewatripont and Rey 1994: 258), or they could specify alternating price announcements and challenges alongside payments to third parties, as the Moore–Repullo mechanism proposes (Moore and Repullo 1988: 1196).

The weakness of these mechanisms is that they each require a strong form of commitment, which is a significant barrier to their usefulness. If the weaker party can refuse the take-it-or-leave-it offer and the stronger party would still trade (which it is mutually rational to do), then the ultimatum is not credible and it will not give the stronger party adequate return on its investment. Likewise, if the parties agree to split the penalty payment to the third party rather than hand it over to that party (again which is mutually rational to do), then the parties do not have an incentive to truthfully announce their valuations prior to the penalty round. Yet, it is unlikely that the parties can credibly commit to actions required for renegotiation design or revelation mechanisms if they cannot make such commitments to the original contract to deter hold-up in the first place.

One way to obtain this commitment, ostensibly without smart contracts and blockchain, is to include penalty clauses – liquidated damages larger than economic damages – if the parties do not comply with the mechanisms (de Geest and Wuyts 2000). For example, the stronger party may have to pay a penalty if it makes a second offer after its take-it-or-leave-it offer is rejected by the weaker party but before the weaker party requests the default trade in the ADR mechanism.[26] Indeed, penalty clauses could go further and possibly

---

[25] With finite period games, the parties have an incentive to hold-up in the last stage. Given this, they will also have it in the penultimate stage, which now looks like the final stage. This process repeats until the value of repeat play evaporates (Gibbons 1992).

[26] In some cases, the penalty clause may have to be paid to a third party, otherwise it might directly undermine the incentives the mechanism set up for the parties. For example, if the penalty for

disincentivize hold-up in the first place by penalizing deviations from the original contract terms, if the parties are comfortable with foregoing any flexibility to depart from the original contract.

The problem with this approach is that courts frown upon penalty clauses, although they may be more permissive in cases where both parties are sophisticated businesses rather than cases involving small businesses or individual consumers (Farnsworth 2003: 845). If courts won't enforce the penalty clause, they will not incentivize parties to commit to their roles in the mechanisms or to their original contract terms.

Even if courts would enforce the penalty clause, it can skew the incentives of the two parties. Such clauses act like reliance damages, which are known to risk overinvestment by the protected parties (Rogerson 1984: 41). The solution to overinvestment is to pay the penalties to a third party rather than the party making an investment. Yet, both contractual parties have a mutual incentive to negotiate around that third-party payment, as they did in the revelation mechanism (Holmstrom 1982: 327, showing that relaxing the budget breaker yields an efficient Nash equilibrium of the moral hazard in a team game).

The only way to obtain commitment without tilting investment incentives then is to have an automatic payment to a third party that cannot be undone by the contractual parties. For example, the parties could set up something akin to a poison pill, where the contract or mechanism creates an IOU from the penalized party to a third party (Dawson et al. 1987). Of course, if there is a gap between the timing of the investment and the payment for that investment, the holding-up party could still petition a court to enjoin the poison pill–type penalty before it is triggered by failure to make payment for the investment. The held-up party is unlikely to invest much to stop the holding-up party because it does not benefit from the payment to a third party.

To avoid both circumvention of the penalty by the parties (directly) and by courts (after being petitioned by the parties) is to have the penalty be something that even the court cannot enjoin. An outlandish but effective solution is to create a machine, have the party that needs to show commitment place a large amount of cash in the machine, then have the machine rigged to burn the cash if that party fails to meet its commitment. The machine must have a dead-hand switch so that it is triggered if anyone – even the court via injunction – tries to shut it down.

This machine must be all-knowing about the parties' accounts, otherwise the parties could get around even this machine. Specifically, they could renegotiate

---

negotiating around the third-party payment in the revelation mechanism is a penalty paid by one of the parties to another, they would simply account for it in their negotiations over the first payment.

but transact in two parts: one that appears to the machine to conform to the original contract, and a second that undoes the original contract and consummates the renegotiated contract. If the machine only observed the first transaction, it would release the cash it was holding hostage even though the second transaction consummated the renegotiated contract. Again, investment incentives would be undermined.

But this machine we have described is hard to build and actually looks very much like a smart contract on blockchain. Moreover, the latter are simple and cheaper to implement. The smart contract is just a computer script, not an awkward physical machine; it can work with digital money, which is easier to obtain than actual cash; and can be made all knowing with application program interfaces (APIs) to all of the parties' accounts (see Section 5). Moreover, blockchain allows irreversible transfers to anonymous accounts.

4 Background on Blockchain and Smart Contracts

We believe blockchain technology, used together with smart contracts, can overcome some of the hurdles to credible commitment in contracts with current contracting technology. In this section, we describe the main value added from blockchain and smart contracts and then explain how these technologies might better enable the sort of contractual commitment required either to stop all renegotiation or to enable the use of renegotiation design or revelation mechanisms, the two strategies for eliminating hold-up.

We also qualify this optimistic assessment by pointing out some of the limitations of blockchain in resolving the hold-up problem, and we distinguish environments where blockchain holds significant promise (such as in financial intermediation), and where it may have real limitations (such as in housing or procurement contracts).

4.1 The Value of Blockchain

Blockchain, a computer science innovation introduced by Satoshi Nakamoto in 2008, is described as a distributed or decentralized, open and secure ledger, meaning that it verifies transactions are intended, feasible and executed through a decentralized system rather than through a central authority (like a government or bank, which might be costly or untrustworthy), it records transactions in a public way (so as to build reputations and counterparty trust) and ensures transactions are not reversible (to protect parties from certain types of theft).[27] Although Nakamoto initially intended the term transaction to mean a monetary

---

[27] Nakamoto is a pseudonym; his or her identity is uncertain (Wikipedia 2021a).

transfer, a transaction recorded in blockchain can be any set of promises – that is, a contract, or indeed any statement (Buterin 2014: 14).

4.1.1 The Core Function of Blockchain Is Witnessing Statements (without Relying on Any One Witness)

A simple analogy clarifies the core function of blockchain. Blockchain – which refers both to the method by which a record of statements is made and to the recorded statements themselves – is akin to a witness. Suppose A and B agree that A will rent an apartment to B for $600/month. We can decompose that agreement into a statement by A that A will give B access to the apartment and by B that B will pay A a given amount per month. To commemorate their transaction, they can each write down these statements on paper and sign those statements. The written statements can serve as proof to third parties that A and B made the statements written down. An alternative is to find a witness. If that witness is a neutral third party, then they can testify credibly to outsiders to the statements that A and B make. Either way, outsiders would be able to more confidently rely on statements from B that they have an apartment that they want to rent out, or from A that they have $600 to spend.[28]

A witness's value – relative to paper statements – is not that they are uniquely credible but that they incrementally improve the credibility of statements and in some cases more cost-effectively enhance such credibility. Certainly, a paper document plus a witness is more credible than just a paper document. Witnesses may also have two advantages over paper documents. In some cases, the witness may be cheaper, because paper documents may require the assistance of costly lawyers to write. The witness also may be more credible, because a paper contract can sometimes be forged. This is not always true: a witness may lie if they are biased in favor of or bribed by one of the parties. But the witness may be better than paper documents in some cases.

Blockchain is simply a new technology to witness transactions. The old-fashioned approach is to have another human, ideally unrelated (or equally related) to the two or more parties to a transaction, observe the transaction. In some cases, it was a central, privileged party, such as the government – for example, when a judge witnesses a wedding, or when a bank validates a check from B to A. In other cases, it was simply an authorized third party, for example, a public notary. In yet other cases, the witnessing is recognized ex post, as required, as when a court admits probative evidence, such as a document that

---

[28] One notable outsider is a court: if there is a dispute over the agreement and the parties go to court, the witness can help the court resolve issues of fact.

was signed by both parties. Blockchain's approach to witnessing is different: it uses cryptographic algorithms mediated by a computer network.

At its base, blockchain sets up a network. Two of the more popular such networks are Bitcoin and Ethereum (Bitinfocharts 2021a, showing that Bitcoin and Ethereum have equal volume, greater than other cryptocurrency platforms). If A and B want to transact, they each announce their transaction to the network. Blockchain sets up a method by which computers on the network, called "nodes," can hear the messages from A and B. The nodes then produce evidence that they heard that message – that is, they validate it (Nakamoto 2008: 2; see also Bitcoin.org 2021).

Technically speaking, the evidence that validates a transaction on a blockchain network is the output from a so-called hash function, a type of one-way function in mathematics.[29] A hash function is an algorithm wherein, upon hearing what A and B say, the node – let's call it W as it serves as a witness – transforms the message into a "hash." (The action of transforming the message is called "hashing.") The key feature of the hash is that people who observe it know that W must have witnessed A and B saying that they were going to give access to an apartment and pay $600/month, respectively. How do they know that? Because hash functions have the property that there is no way for W to produce its hash unless it heard A and B say that they were going to give access to an apartment and pay $600/month, respectively. In other words, one of the inputs to the hash function is the announced transaction and the output is a hash that validates that the transaction was indeed announced (Antonopolous 2017: 227–228).

Once the network produces evidence of a transaction – that is, the hash – it is added to a list of previously witnessed transactions. The whole list is called the blockchain, so sometimes people say they "add the hash to the blockchain"

---

[29] A one-way function is a function where if you know the inputs, you can produce the outputs, but if you only have the outputs, you cannot know for sure the inputs (Antonopolous 2017: 56). An example is $2 + 3 = 5$. The inputs are 2 and 3 and the function is addition. The output is 5. If you know 2 and 3, you know the output of addition is 5. But if you know only 5, you cannot know whether the inputs are 2 and 3 or any of the following pairs: (0,5), (5,0), (1,4), (4,1), (3,2).

Addition is not the best one-way function for blockchain, as it is also desirable to have a situation where only when A and B present 2 and 3 can they prove that they were the ones that spoke. With addition, A and B could come forward and say that they said 1 and 4, and it too would be validated since the sum is 5. So, the one-way functions are both a one-way and unique mapping from inputs to outputs. A better example than addition is prime factorization, which is actually used in cryptography. If I give you number X and ask you the fewest number of primes that, when multiplied together, yield X, you have a problem that rises quickly in complexity as X increases. If I tell you a series of primes, you can easy calculate its product X; but if I just give you X, it is very difficult to calculate its prime factorization.

A form of one-way functions used often with blockchain are trap-door functions. These are one-way functions such that, if you have some secret information (i.e., know the "trap-door"), you can compute the inputs from the outputs.

(Nakamoto 2008: 2; Bitcoin.org 2021). Because the blockchain is a list of transactions, it is also called a ledger (Antonopolous 2017: 2; Blockgeeks. com 2021a).

4.1.2 Blockchain Is an Open Ledger to Take Advantage of the Economies of Scale from Witnessing

Blockchain is often described as a public, distributed ledger. The distributed portion refers to the method of witnessing, which we just described, but the open ledger portion of this refers to the fact that the blockchain is publicly available (Iansiti and Lakhani 2017: p. 2703). The reason it is open is that there are economies of scale from witnessing.

By economies of scale in witnessing, we mean that the value of witnessing two transactions is worth more than witnessing just one transaction. To see why that is, consider our rental transaction: A gives B rights to an apartment and B gives A \$600/month. Suppose C wants to sublease the apartment. If C is able to observe that A gave B rights to the apartment, C is more confident that B has rights to the apartment that C wants. Of course, the fact that potential counterparties benefit from observing A and B's exchange just means that witnessing A and B's exchange is valuable. To show economies, we must show that D, who wants to use the apartment C has for a weekend in an Airbnb-type transaction, benefits not only from seeing B's transfer to C but also A's transfer to B. That is certainly the case: seeing A give B the apartment gives D confidence that B had an apartment to give to C. In other words, being able to observe multiple transactions increases a party's confidence that their counterparty actually has the asset that is to be transferred to the party. There are economies because once A and B's transaction is observed and publicly validated on the blockchain, it can be used both by C and, without additional cost, by D.[30]

A necessary condition for witnessing to have economies of scale is that the validation be made public and that ownership be traceable across transactions. To reduce transaction costs, the public validation should be maintained in a database where public validation of other related transactions is maintained. So, the feature of blockchain that achieves these economies of scale is that it is publicly searchable (Antonopolous 2017: 16, 147).

Earlier we said that the core function of blockchain is witnessing rather than public reporting. We said that in part because blockchain without witnessing is just an open database, like the title registry that tracks land ownership. It is

---

[30] Of course, there is a marginal cost to D of processing the information about A and D. We ignore this as that cost is the same regardless of how the information about A and B is generated.

witnessing that gives entries into the database value. In the last section, we noted blockchain is an open database.

4.1.3 Security and the Inalterability of Blockchain

A feature that distinguishes a blockchain public database of transactions from other public databases of transactions is that there are so-called consensus rules. With a traditional database, a central authority is charged with making sure the database is not retroactively modified to reallocate ownership of items. If the centralized authority is untrustworthy – for example, if it is also a participant in transactions recorded on the database or it accepts side payments from participants to modify the database – then the database's credibility is compromised (Antonopolous 2017: 217). With a blockchain database, there need not be any central administrator of the database. Anyone can contribute an entry. But what stops anyone from also modifying old transactions (perhaps to benefit themselves or harm competitors)? Each blockchain network has a consensus rule that determines when a database can be updated and therefore also retroactively modified (Antonopolous 2017: 26).

The most common consensus rule is proof-of-work validation, in which nodes compete to be the first to hash an announced transaction and the winner is the first to add the transaction to the blockchain (Nakamoto 2008: 3; Bitcoin. org 2021). This method requires a node to deploy central processing unit (CPU) time (i.e., electricity and a CPU) to perform hash functions and thereby validate transactions. To change a past transaction, a node has to employ enough CPU time to modify an old transaction and revalidate all other transactions, including new transactions that are occurring in the interim. This requires a lot more CPU time; indeed, Nakamoto (2008: 6–7) showed that it requires that no one node controls a majority of all CPU power on the blockchain network.

Although proof-of-work makes retroactive modification of the blockchain hard, it also makes validation of new transactions hard. By hard, we mean it consumes a lot of electricity (Buterin 2016). An important alternative method being explored is proof-of-stake. Under proof-of-stake, transactions are validated by betting that they are correct. Nodes put up money that the transaction that they state occurred actually occurred. If others put up more money to say that the transaction did not occur, then the node betting on the transaction loses the money that said that the transaction occurred (Buterin 2016). Other alternatives include other methods of voting for which transaction actually occurred, with the alternatives being differentiated by the weight that each node's vote has (Baliga 2017; Castor 2017). With alternatives to proof-of-work, the manner in which transactions are validated should be chosen so as to balance the goal of reducing the cost of incentives to validate truthful transactions and of increasing the cost of incentives to retroactively modify past recorded transactions.

4.1.4 Anonymity and Privacy on the Blockchain

Another feature that makes blockchain attractive to some[31] is that blockchain can preserve anonymity or promote privacy. This is done in either of two ways. One is by disassociating accounts with personal identities on the blockchain database. For example, people may just have public identification numbers, also called public keys, and those keys are not associated with names, addresses or other identification numbers easily connected to names or addresses (Antonopolous 2017: 57). It should be noted, however, that various governments have imposed know-your-customer (KYC) rules on exchanges that facilitate transactions on blockchains and these can make it harder to maintain anonymity on the blockchain (Althauser 2017). A second way to ensure privacy is to create and maintain a private blockchain that is only accessible to a small number of participants or that can only be searched by a centralized intermediary, who can validate whether counterparties have certain assets or not (Laurence 2017: 8).

Both methods of limiting public knowledge of transactions, unsurprisingly, limit the economies of scale from blockchain. As a result, blockchain networks must balance the returns to scale with the value of privacy when choosing how they will be constructed.

4.2 The Value of Smart Contracts

So-called smart contracts, as first conceived by Nick Szabo (2021), are a quite general concept: a smart contract is a simple series of actions written in computer script.[32] When the actions constitute fulfillment of mutual, conditional promises, they are a contract in the traditional sense.[33] Smart contracts can fully or partially specify a contract, meaning that they can include all promises made pursuant to a contract or they can contain part of the promises, in which case the code plus a paper agreement constitute the whole contract (Stark 2016).

---

[31] This includes individuals trading in illegal goods, such as the seller on the Silk Road website, individuals facing capital controls and individuals facing the risk of expropriation by governments or instability in their countries.

[32] An example of a scripted contract on the Ethereum network is available at www.ethereum.org /token.

[33] Indeed, smart contracts can be used to create not only real-world contracts but also real-world corporations. One of the original smart contracts on the Ethereum network was a decentralized autonomous organization (DAO). A DAO is a set of smart contracts that specify the governance, assets and liabilities of a group of people or nodes on a network (Allison 2016).

Smart contracts can exist independent of a blockchain network, but they can also be announced, witnessed and automatically executed on such a network. Indeed, the reason Vitalik Buterin (2014) created the Ethereum network was that the Bitcoin network did not sufficiently support smart contracts. Ethereum is a blockchain network but with a scripting language that allows smart contracts. Individuals write their smart contracts in that language and the Ethereum network validates and executes it.

4.2.1 Benefits That Smart Contracts Do Not Offer

What makes smart contracts special is not that they are automated. One can already automate transactions. Take the case where A rents an apartment to B for $600/month. With a smart contract, simply by signing the contract would B automate the process of paying A because their account on the blockchain network would be deducted $600/month – but B could have done that before smart contracts. For example, they could have signed a paper rental agreement and then set up a standing order at their bank to send A an e-check for $600/month.[34]

Of course, there are fewer steps with a smart contract, which could reduce transaction costs with contract execution. Writing and digitally signing a smart contract script could, in theory, eliminate the need to take extra steps to automate the process (Stark 2016).

But this benefit is offset by the fact that automation via smart contract requires the smart contract to be on a network that controls enough of A and B's assets to be able to be completely self-executing on that network. For example, if B writes their smart contract on the Ethereum network but does not have wealth in an Ethereum network account, then they would have to transfer money to an Ethereum account to empower Ethereum to direct it according to the contract. If all B did was to allow an Ethereum network to check their regular bank account, the smart contract could not execute the contract.

Nor do smart contracts obviously reduce transaction costs during contract drafting. Traditional contracts require the parties and/or a lawyer to draft a contract, but smart contracts require the parties and/or a hired programmer to script those contracts. Services like Legal Zoom (www.legalzoom.com) can help with form contracts, but form contracts can be used to economize with traditional paper contracts as well as script contracts.

So, what are the benefits of smart contracts over ordinary contracts?

---

[34] This is similar to the example used by Blockgeeks.com to illustrate what a smart contract is (Blockgeeks.com 2021b).

4.2.2 Smart Contracts Reduce Uncertainty about Promises (Counterparty Risk)

A smart contract, by virtue of being a plan for the future and being automated, gives counterparties confidence that promises will be fulfilled. Take our rental example. Even if B sets up an automatic payment for $600/month to A with their bank, there is a risk that the payment will not be made. To see why, suppose B only has $600 in their account on September 29 and rent is due October 1. If B decides to have dinner out on the 29th that costs $25, the bank will not be able to transfer $600 on the 1st. B will be $25 short. By contrast, a smart contract can be written so that their account encumbers the $600 even before the 1st so that B cannot spend $25 on dinner on the 29th if they only has $600 in the account that day (Stark 2016).[35]

An inexact analogy to the smart contract counterparty is a secured creditor. A secured creditor knows that, even if the debtor cannot pay their debts even after litigation or bankruptcy, the creditor can seize their collateral – for example, a home that secures a mortgage. By contrast, an unsecured creditor whose debtor cannot pay even after litigation or bankruptcy may get nothing. A smart contract payee can be sure that their counterparty will not otherwise spend or encumber the money that they expect to be paid under the smart contract. By contrast, an ordinary contract payee faces the risk that their counterparty will not have the money to pay, leaving them with the same recourse as the unsecured creditor. Of course, the ordinary contract payee can try to obtain a security interest, but that just means that smart contracts and security interests are substitutes, underlining our point that the two are roughly analogous.

When combined with an open database of transactions, such as that maintained by a blockchain network, smart contracts can disproportionately reduce counterparty risk in the economy. To illustrate, let us complicate the rental example by allowing that B must earn income each month to pay rent. Specifically, on the 1st of the month, B's account, which had $600 falls to $0, but B expects to get a biweekly paycheck of $1,000 (net of taxes). To address the risk that B's biweekly paycheck may not arrive – for example, because they are demoted or takes unpaid leave – the smart contract could include an algorithm that predicts income and, on that basis, encumbers the account to protect rent payments. When income is more uncertain, the encumbrance should be larger to ensure a given level of confidence, say 95 percent, that

---

[35] It is easy to complicate this example to account for interest. With interest at a rate of r per day, the smart contract would simply require B to have $600/(1 + r)^2 < 600$ rather than 600 in her account on September 29.

rent payments would be made on time. Indeed, the rental contract price itself could – and from A's perspective should – be a function of how predictable B's income is. This means that, if B's employer also signed a smart contract, B's income would also become more secure and they would have to pay A less for rent! In this manner, the more smart contracts spread, the more limited counterparty risk is, and the less insurance – in the form of higher prices – needs to be purchased against that risk. The money freed up by lower insurance payments could be spent on investment, which should increase growth.

4.2.3 Smart Contracts Reduce Uncertainty about Interpretation (Legal Risk)

A second source of risk that smart contracts can address is interpretation risk. When two parties write a traditional contract, there may be ambiguities in meaning. Those ambiguities are subsequently resolved by a court or equivalent adjudicator. But from an ex ante perspective, that resolution is still risky (Torbert 2017).

We can illustrate with a simple example. Suppose that A and B write a paper contract on Monday that says

> A will supply B a widget on Friday. B will pay $100 upon delivery of the widget. If A does not perform, A owes B $150.

Suppose further that on Tuesday a hurricane strikes, destroying A's factory and inventory, so that they cannot perform on the smart contract. If B sues A in state court for liquidated damages, a court could decide in at least two ways. First, the court could say that the contract has an implied force majeure clause, perhaps because that is what the parties would have agreed to if they had considered the possibility of a hurricane while writing their contract, and so A did not breach and owes B nothing. Second, the court could say that the four corners of the contract includes no force majeure clause, so A did breach and owes B $150.

When writing the contract, each party formed an expectation about what a court would do, and accounted for that expectation in the price upon which they agreed. If one of the parties was risk averse, the price might have to reflect insurance provided to that party to insure it against the risk from court interpretation (not just the risk of a hurricane). If the parties disagreed on what would happen, they might not agree on a price. If, for example, A's expectation about the cost of supplying a widget was greater than B's expectation about the probability of getting the widget times the value of the widget to be, there would be no range for bargaining. In short, if the parties were risk averse or if the parties disagreed about what a court would do, it would be more likely that the parties would not come to an agreement.

A smart contract can reduce the interpretation risk. Because a computer interprets a script like a strictly textualist court would – that is, it looks only at the four corners of the contract – the outcome may be more predictable than when a court's interpretive methodology is uncertain. In fact, it is possible to do even better than a strictly textualist court because it is possible to cheaply and quickly simulate and thus predict how a computer would execute a smart contract script under a wide array of parameter values for contract inputs (Blockgeeks.com 2021b, citing Marino 2015).

Anyone who has written code might object that code is very finicky, but this is a negligible cost. For example, a misplaced semi-colon might cause the smart contract to not execute at all, but one can test the contract in a sandbox[36] and see if it executes even before it is actually executed in a live environment.

A potentially stronger objection is that the parties might not have intended the meaning of the four corners of the smart contract, but even this is not compelling. The parties can write a different script. Alternatively, default rule code can be written that fills gaps in smart contracts and the parties can reference that default rule code when scripting their contract. In other words, they can't pick the interpretive methodology, but they can pick their default rules.

The magnitude of the benefit from reducing interpretive risk, like the magnitude of the benefit of reducing counterparty risk is uncertain. While the former may be smaller than the latter, it could still be significant. The former may be what drives contractual parties to agree to assign jurisdiction or arbitrate decisions or to move transactions within a firm (Gruson 1980). Most consumer contracts have arbitration clauses and half of all trade occurs within firms (Antràs 2003; Tidmarsh 2015). Reduced interpretive and counterparty risks are not the only reason why the parties may use arbitration clauses or prefer intrafirm transactions, but they are significant risks. Indeed, counterparty risk is what spawned the creation of blockchain in the first place.[37]

5 How Smart Contracts on Blockchain Can Help Reduce Contractual Hold-up

Our central claim is that smart contracts on blockchain networks allow parties to more credibly commit to original contracts (in case they want to prevent any

---

[36] A sandbox is a software developer term for a simulated environment where code can be tested to see if it works or what its impacts might be before it is actually deployed in the real world (Wikipedia 2021b).

[37] Bitcoin, the first application of blockchain, was created to solve the double spending problem (Nakamoto 2008: 1).

renegotiation) or to mechanisms to structure renegotiation or make information verifiable to courts (in case they want specifically to stop hold-up). Here we explain how practically to do that. The implementation we suggest requires some assumptions and we will clarify those as well.

5.1 An Example with the ADR Renegotiation Design Mechanism

Suppose that Apple and Corning wish to write a contract that includes an ADR mechanism to structure renegotiation after a hold-up so that the hold-up does not deter efficient relationship-specific investment. Recall that the ADR mechanism requires one party be given a default option and the other the credibility to make a take-it-or-leave-it offer. Each requires commitment– that is, the latter party must have strong incentives not to a second offer and the former a strong incentive not to renegotiate the default offer. How could the parties implement this with these new technologies?

Learning from Section 2.5.1, we would first ask how much information the parties have. If it is enough to devise a renegotiation design or revelation mechanism, then the parties would want to construct a penalty provision that deters deviation from the mechanism and that cannot be undone by courts or the parties through renegotiation. If the amount of information is not adequate to devise such mechanisms, the only thing that the parties can do is construct a penalty provision that discourages any deviation from the original contract. Of course, such a penalty provision would also bar renegotiation due honestly to changed circumstances and that does not affect ex ante incentives to invest. So the parties should not construct a penalty that locks in the original contract unless the expected cost of hold-up is greater than the expected cost of inflexibility.

To illustrate how a penalty clause could be constructed, suppose the parties have enough information to write an ADR renegotiation design mechanism. Let's see how the penalty provision would work. First, we examine the default option. In our example, it is Corning that is to be given the option to trade a unit with probability 5/6 at price 23 1/3. We would script a clause in the smart contract code that says Corning can ask for the default trade and if that trade is not consummated, then Apple pays a penalty. Likewise, the smart contract code would make Apple pay a penalty if it communicated a second offer to Corning after Corning refused its first ostensibly take-it-or-leave-it offer.

In order not to skew the incentives of the parties when playing the ADR game, the penalty must flow to a third party. For instance, if the smart contract does not observe the default trade by a certain time or if it observes a second offer from Apple, then the code would irreversibly transfer money from Apple to anonymous third parties.

Blockchain makes it possible for penalties to flow to third parties. All the smart contract has to do is specify that some large amount would be transferred from Apple's account (its public address or key) on the network to a randomly generated list of public addresses or keys and that the smart contract would announce to the blockchain network the private keys associated with those public keys. The latter step would allow any node on the network to access and transfer to their account the money at those public addresses. It would be as if the code announced that there was a pile of cash on the corner of Broadway and Fifth Avenue in Manhattan: people would rush to take the money (Antonopolous 2017: 17, explaining how transferring money to a public key for which the private key is publicly known would lead to loss of funds). The entities that collect the money distributed by the smart contract would be able to remain anonymous – as blockchain allows anonymous transactions (Aru 2017). If that entity were located in a country that did not have a KYC requirement, they could also convert that money into the government currency of their choice. There are plenty of countries happy to do that (US Department of State 2012; PWC 2013; IRS 2021).

The penalized party, and perhaps even the nonpenalized party, would have an incentive to go to court to enjoin the penalty. With the default option, Apple would have an incentive to not be penalized for defying Corning's request. With Apple's take-it-or-leave-it offer, Apple has an ex post incentive to avoid the penalty for making a second offer and Corning has an incentive to receive a second Apple offer, meaning both would want to petition a court.

The future commitment feature of smart contracts and the irreversibility of blockchain transactions can render court injunctions ineffective. Once the parties sign the agreement, future exchanges are already booked and cannot be undone – by either the parties or a court – without having either a majority of the computing power or the tokens on the blockchain (see Section 4.1.3). A court does not have that. Thus, a court can no more require a transaction on blockchain be reversed than it can require that the stock price of a company that committed fraud increase to compensate shareholders.

Court-ordered damages would not help undermine the smart contract commitment. For one thing, punishing Corning because Apple has to pay a penalty does not change Apple's incentives unless Corning has to pay Apple to compensate for the penalty Apple must pay. But if Corning has to pay Apple, then the penalty script in the smart contract can make the penalty contingent on subsequent damages ordered by a court. For example, if the optimal penalty on Apple for, say, making more than one offer is 100 and the damages awarded by the court for making Apple pay a penalty is D, the script could say Apple must pay 100 + D.

Apple may be tempted to hold Corning up but avoid penalties by renegotiating in two steps. First, they would comply with the ADR mechanism in the original contract. Second, they would simultaneously write a separate contract with Corning that functionally puts Apple in the same position as if it had successfully held up Corning in the original contracts. This second contract would say that Corning will sell to Apple one unit of Gorilla glass at a price that is equal to the price the parties would negotiate for Gorilla glass in the abstract (say p_2) minus an amount equal to how much a successful hold-up in the original contract would benefit Apple. This benefit is equal to the difference between the price that the original contract specified (p_1) and the price Apple could extract if it was able successfully to hold Corning up ($p_H < p_1$). In short, the second contract price would be $p_2 - (p_1 - p_H)$.

Blockchain can be used to prevent renegotiating through subsequent contracts as well. The smart contract could crudely specify that, if there were a second exchange between Apple and Corning, the penalty would be triggered. Of course, that approach would have collateral damage: the parties may reasonably want to trade a second time and this penalty trigger would prevent that. To address that, the parties could agree that the penalty would only be triggered if the second contract had a lower price than the first contract, although this would create problems if Corning's costs fell over time. Alternatively, they could even configure the smart contract to both structure renegotiation on the first trade and to provide a framework for subsequent trades.[38] That framework includes a revelation mechanism for subsequent trades that would allow the smart contract to compare the price and cost of the subsequent trades to ensure that Corning was fully reimbursed for its investment in prior to the first trade.

A natural question is how the smart contract code would know if Corning or Apple violated the default option or final offer or negotiated a subsequent contract that de facto renegotiated their original contract. The smart contract can certainly monitor the blockchain – the ledger of transactions – on the network, in which case it would know directly if another trade occurs. It is here that the open feature of blockchain is critical. It could also monitor communications or accounts not on the blockchain network by using APIs that gave it access to the parties' messages or to other accounts the parties may have.[39] When the parties sign the contract, they want the penalties so that

---

[38] This is not uncommon in long-term contracts where the end date is not specified (López-Bayón and González-Díaz 2010).

[39] See https://plaId.com/ for an example of how this might work. For more information on other similar services, see this thread on stack overflow: https://stackoverflow.com/questions/

they would have an incentive to allow the smart contract access to all their messages and accounts.[40]

Of course, the fact that the parties want to share information does not mean it is easy to do so. It may be difficult to give access to all communications between parties, for example, in person conversations between employees of the two parties.[41] It may also be that the parties have accounts at some banks that do not provide APIs that can give the smart contract access and the parties cannot change those banks' policies. We hope this is a limitation that recedes in time as more accounts become interoperable in the sense of providing API access. We also think it may not be a large limitation as parties certainly have an incentive to keep most of their money in accounts with banks that offer APIs, as those APIs allow the parties themselves to monitor their own accounts more easily.

5.2 Generalizing the Example

Having shown examples of how ADR provisions might be implemented, we can infer how the provisions required for a revelation mechanism or the original contract as a whole can be implemented via smart contract. The smart contract can employ penalties to get the parties to comply with specific steps of the revelation mechanism. To complete each mechanism, the smart contracts must require that parties take actions in a certain sequence, for example, the take-it-or-leave-it offer comes before the default option can be triggered, otherwise the party that was not supposed to move faces penalties. Since the renegotiation design mechanism is the whole contract, the parties that want to employ that mechanism need only specify the steps that that mechanism requires. Parties that wish to employ the revelation mechanism can only finalize their smart contract by adding to their revelation mechanism a schedule of contingent trades that are each triggered by a different combination of valuations v and costs c revealed through the revelation mechanism.

7269668/is-there-an-api-to-get-bank-transaction-and-bank-balance (noting that Yodlee.com and Mint.com do the same, though banks may charge to access the API).

[40] If one of the parties did not, then the other party would not want to enter the contract with that party. As a result, the party that considered not giving access would give access because ex ante they would benefit from the contract, even at the cost of giving access. Especially since access to the smart contract is not the same as public access, as the smart contract would not share the messages or account information with anyone, even counterparties.

[41] Various email providers, for example, Google, allow API access to email, but typically only for the owner of the account, not third parties, including smart contracts. For google, see https://developers.google.com/gmail/api/; for a general example, see also https://blog.context.io/. However, if there is demand for this, there is no technical barrier to it. In any case, the account owner can provide the smart contract script this power. This is no different than an IFTTT (acronym for "if this then that") script that signals to third parties the actions of an account owner. For IFTTT examples with Gmail as an input, see https://ifttt.com/gmail.

For those parties that do not have the relevant information to devise renegotiation design or revelation mechanisms, blockchain still has value. Such parties have to make a choice: write a contract that never allows renegotiation, or always allows renegotiation, whether due to hold-up or to changed circumstances. If they think the hold-up problem is bigger than the problem of inflexibility, they can bar renegotiation under any circumstance by imposing penalties for such renegotiation. The steps were outlined earlier.

5.3 Robustness of Smart Contracts on the Blockchain

Smart contracts on the blockchain have at least three limitations that we have not yet discussed. One is that government may simply ban blockchain or smart contracts that impose penalties.[42] This seems like an extreme course of action and, while we can only speculate, this does not seem particularly likely. Blockchain has a great deal of value outside of the contractual commitment setting. Entities that obtain that value would likely lobby or litigate against a broad ban of blockchain (Matonis 2013). A narrower ban on smart contracts with penalties is perhaps more plausible. It would be akin to a ban on penalty clauses (Farnsworth 2003: 845). The main problem is that the ban is difficult to enforce. Both parties to a contract with a penalty want that penalty ex ante, so have little incentive to report that they have written a smart contract with a penalty. And ex post a court would face difficulties in rescuing them from that penalty if the penalty is written correctly or if the parties remain anonymous – as discussed earlier.

One possibility is that KYC rules – versions of which already exist – could be used to pierce the anonymity of the contracting parties. Then the efficacy of the smart contract would hinge on whether courts are willing to enforce contracts that fully ensure one or both of the contracting parties against decisions by the court. Courts may well blanch at such provisions and refuse to enforce them. This would limit the applicability and efficacy of the smart contracts that we have outlined.

Absent this, only a whistleblower, a third party, or a contractual party who was coerced into agreeing to a smart contract penalty clause has an incentive to get courts involved. But legislators would have to authorize bounties for whistleblowers, another type of third-party standing, or criminal penalties. Those may be political hard sells because no outsiders are hurt by the commitment described in this element. The biggest risk comes from coerced parties. Indeed, these are the individuals who were able to undermine penalty clauses in

---

[42] See, for example, Lee (2017), noting that China has shut down cryptocurrency exchanges. However, this does not mean all blockchain networks are banned in China.

non-smart contracts. Perhaps the difficulty of enforcing a ban on all smart contracts with penalty causes will give courts an opportunity to limit their ban on such agreements to those where one of the parties is unsophisticated and may have been coerced into signing it.

A second limitation concern with smart contracts on blockchain is that, like computer scripts generally, they are sensitive to honest mistakes. For example, if Apple accidentally hits send on its email that contains a draft – but not the final draft – of its take-it-or-leave-it offer, the smart contract will not allow it to recall the message, otherwise Apple could circumvent the smart contract by calling its first offer a message it wants to recall. To address the costs of such mistakes, game theorists sometimes look for equilibria of games that are robust to "trembling hands"; correlatively, mechanism designers might look for game rules that yield trembling hands perfect or robust equilibria (Selten 1975: 38). We do not know if the mechanisms we have discussed in this Element are robust to errors, although empirical work by Aghion et al. (2017: 232) gives us some hope that smaller mistakes might yield smaller deviations from the first best incentives to invest.

It is also possible that even sophisticated parties could simply make a mistake in crafting the smart contract and then find it impossible or extremely costly to reverse. If there is a Pareto improvement to be made from correcting the smart contract, then both parties would have an incentive to renegotiate the contract and reveal themselves to the court. This presents important challenges for how courts should respond to such circumstances. On the one hand, it would be unusual for a court to stand in the way of an agreement that makes both parties better off. On the other hand, refusing to do so might deter the use of smart contracts in general. Indeed, if the court wishes to deter such contracts, it may want to develop doctrine that does just that by being unwilling to correct mistakes at the request of the parties to the smart contract.

Another way to frame this drawback with smart contracts is that they introduce a new form of transaction cost – namely the cost of blockchain adaptation. This suggests a clear trade-off between the benefits of commitment and the costs of being unable to adapt (easily) to changing circumstances. One would naturally expect that in environments where adapting to changing circumstances is very important that smart contracts on a blockchain would be less desirable, and used less extensively.

A third limitation of the smart contract penalties is that they only work if the parties have sufficient assets to pay the penalties required by the smart contract. One way to ensure that smart contract penalties can be implemented and are effective is for the parties to place enough assets in their accounts on the blockchain network to cover penalties until both parties satisfactorily perform on the contract. Note that these assets are available to be employed or spent until penalties are required if the parties take out a loan collateralized by the assets in their account on the blockchain. Another way to ensure penalties can be covered is to not require the parties to put up a bond on the blockchain but to allow the smart contract to create debt on behalf of the penalized party to a lender, with the proceeds from the lender being used to pay third parties pursuant to the penalty. The lender would be willing to do so long as the party on the hook for the penalty had enough assets, on the blockchain or otherwise. Of course, if either party did not have enough assets to cover optimal penalties, optimal penalties would not be available. In that case, penalties would have to be lowered, and hold-up risks would rise commensurately.

A final potential limitation of smart contracts concerns implementation. As we mentioned earlier in this Element, the automated execution facilitated by smart contracts takes as a crucial input information that can be verified digitally. As Bakos and Halaburda (2019) point out, this information will often come from the so-called Internet of Things. They put it this way: "IoT sensors expand the state space over which the contract can be specified by creating finer partitions of the verifiable states of nature. This typically leads to more efficient trades, but it is still not fully efficient." Indeed, the proximity of what we call the smart-contract second best to the first-best outcome will be a function of the information required by the first-best contract and the efficacy of the information-providing technology. Indeed, this technological view of the second-best is a nascent and interesting area for future work.

6 Conclusion

In this Element, we have highlighted the problem of hold-up, a specific type of transaction cost that can reduce parties' incentives to make relationship-specific investments or to trade in the first place. We argued that traditional contracts, made on paper and enforced with existing financial technology and litigation strategies, cannot provide the very high level of commitment necessary to limit the harms from hold-up. Finally, we explained that smart contracts on blockchain networks have features that, when these technologies become widely deployed, may be able to provide a greater degree of commitment and thus additional protection against hold-up.

We have also emphasized some of the issues concerning the robustness of smart contracts and ways in which such contracts may be "undone" by courts. The degree to which this is a limitation on using smart contracts to address the hold-up problem depends on both the doctrines that courts develop regarding contracts that contain self-executing penalty clauses and which seek to insure the parties against court-ordered outcomes, and the features of the economic environment in which the contracting takes place.

We conclude by considering the implications of our argument for the size of firms, and offer some thoughts about the benefits of smart contracts and blockchain for contract law more generally.

6.1 Implications for Size of Firms

One implication of our claim is that blockchain and smart contracts have to the potential to increase the gains from, and thus amount of, relationship-specific investment and trade and thus total output that we observe in the economy (Williamson 1979). The degree of benefit is proportional to the extent to which hold-up is a drag on investment and trade. In addition, we expect that blockchain should reduce the size of firms. As blockchain increases the returns to market-mediated transactions, firms will move more transactions outside of the firm to the market. In this way, it functions much like prior technological innovations that increased counterparty trust and accountability (Coase 1937; for an example of how technology can have this effect, see Baker and Hubbard 2004). Blockchain may also do this by reducing the role of trust intermediaries, such as banks, in the economy, although that is not a feature we emphasize in this element (Antonopolous 2017: 4).

6.2 Speculation about Effects on Contracting Generally

While our focus has been how smart contracts on the blockchain can tackle the problem of hold-up in contracts, there may be other benefits of these technologies to contract law generally. One that we think is particularly important is that they may reduce the need for centralized entities, especially courts, to resolve contractual disputes. We think this is possible through at least two channels. First, as we explained in Section 5, smart contracts can reduce the need for court interpretation of contracts. A smart contract script, like other computer code, does what it does. The language compiler is the interpreter and it does not permit variation in interpretation. Parties can tackle bugs in the code via simulation, but they get what the code does. In some sense, the compiler is the ultimate textualist interpreter, with little regard for absurdities. Parties do not have to use it, but they have the option. When they do, the role of courts will decline to a greater or lesser extent.

Second, blockchain networks may use their validation mechanism or their consensus rules to adjudicate smart contract disputes. If a smart contract crashes because it is poorly written or if a party feels the counterparty somehow did not honor a smart contract,[43] the network can appoint a third-party node on the network not just to witness the contract but to adjudicate the dispute. The idea would be that, just as the Bitcoin network replaced banks as the intermediary for payments, it can replace courts as arbiters of smart contract disputes.

Of course, the difficulty is that the work required to adjudicate smart contract disputes may not be as algorithmic as mediating transactions. The latter require only that the third party verify the sender of money has enough money in its account (which is evident from the blockchain ledger up until the date of payment) and that the transfer to the receiver's account is recorded in the updated blockchain ledger. Resolving contract disputes requires, for example, determining what the parties would have scripted if they had considered the state in which the smart contract crashed. This requires fact finding beyond the information already available on the blockchain.

It is not clear that other nodes, or even a consensus among nodes, is a good way to resolve the problems. The cost of fact finding of the sort required for adjudication is greater than the cost of fact finding required to verify a payment. The third-party node has to be compensated for that higher cost, just as it is compensated for verifying transactions. Moreover, the other nodes may not be well qualified to adjudicate disputes. The idea of using blockchain is not entirely ludicrous, however. Civil trials, including contract trials, in existing courts also impose great costs on parties. Moreover, they may be tried by a jury, which also may not be qualified.

Even if a blockchain-mediated peer-to-peer network does not displace courts, it may be able to complement courts in two ways. First, it may help courts better identify majoritarian default rules. The more that smart contracts are written on the blockchain, the easier it would be for courts to determine true majoritarian default rules. This is currently difficult as selection into litigation determines what judges see (Baker and Malani 2014: 1577) and general fact finding is limited or biased by the adversarial process (Tarver Robertson 2010: 177). As a result, there is reason to suspect that courts may not be filling in gaps in contracts with the right default rule, but because contracts on the blockchain may be public, the court can directly query what most parties want in specific situations.[44]

Second, just as parties now can set the jurisdiction that will govern their contract disputes, smart contracts may even allow parties to specify which set of (scripted) default rules should govern the gaps in their contracts. This process would be similar to the way in which people putting up intellectual property (IP)

---

[43] For example, perhaps the counterparty negotiated around it off the blockchain.

[44] This is not actually perfect because, even if everyone makes their contracts public, there may be selection into who actually writes provisions that covers specific circumstances. However, it is true that blockchain reduces one layer of selection – namely selection into litigation.

such as photos or images onto the web might simply appeal to the Creative Commons license to govern the usage of their IP. This would lower the demand for courts, but in case disputes that go to trial, it would help courts decide cases.

6.3 The Importance of Blockchain and Smart Contracts

With many new technologies that come along, there is a wave of articles that claim the technology fundamentally changes law. They risk creating what Judge Easterbrook called the law of the horse (Easterbrook 1996). We do not yet think that blockchain and smart contracts will change contract law. Rather, we think it may have a measurable impact on the sorts and amounts of contracts that can be written. To justify our beliefs, we need only to point to the substantial amount of investment going into blockchain. A large fraction of the largest banks, IT companies, and consulting firms are investing in blockchain.[45] The total number and value of transactions on the Bitcoin and Ethereum networks, while still far short of even Paypal, are growing rapidly (Bitinfocharts.com 2012a, 2012b; Altcointoday.com 2017). Finally, the total amount of money raised through initial coin offerings exceeded the total amount of venture funding in the last quarter (Kharpal 2017). While we do not think that there is enough data to conclude that blockchain will change the world, let alone law, we do think that there is enough activity in the technology to begin considering the legal implications of this technology, including, as we do in this article, how blockchain and smart contracts affect contracting.

---

[45] This includes Bank of America Merrill Lynch, Wells Fargo, Citigroup, TD Bank, BBVA, Bank of New York Mellon, Northern Trust, HSBC, Barclays, UBS, Intel and Temasek, which are part of the R3 consortium (Crossman 2017); Accenture, American Express, Cisco, Diamler, Fujitsu, IBM, NEC, and SAP in the Hyperledger consortium (see www.hyperledger.org/members); and BBVA, BP, Deloitte, ING, Infosys, J. P. Morgan, Mastercard, Microsoft, Samsung, Santander, Scotiabank, Thomson Reuters and UBS, which are part of the Enterprise Ethereum alliance (see https://entethalliance.org/members/).

Appendix A
Addressing Hold-up with Options Contracts

Noldeke and Schmidt (1995: 168–171) show that certain option contracts can also achieve the social optimum. Their reasoning is as follows.[46]

The first step is for the buyer and seller to design the renegotiation bargaining game. Here, Noldecke and Schmidt (1995: 165) adopt the following formulation that was first contained in Hart and Moore (1988).

After v and c have been realized, suppose the buyer and seller can simultaneously send each other new offers. Each offer (from each party) is a pair of prices: one if there is trade and one if there is no trade. Trade is assumed to be verifiable by a third party such as a court, and thus the specified payment can be enforced. Said payment is the default, unless one of the parties decides to furnish the court with the new offer from the other party. In equilibrium, only two offers will be furnished: (i) the seller accepting a higher price; or (ii) the buyer accepting a lower price.

Now, suppose the seller receives some default payment, d, if no trade occurs, but has the option to deliver the good to the buyer and receive an additional payment, p, so that the total transfer, t, results in $t = d + p$. The question is how renegotiation works. There are three different cases to consider.

First, suppose that p is less that "low c." If there is no renegotiation, clearly the seller does not want to trade because no matter what the production cost is they will receive less than that amount from the buyer. But if the buyer's valuation is high and the seller's cost is low, then there are gains from trade, and thus renegotiation should occur. Raising p to "low c" will be sufficient to do this, and the buyer does not need to go any higher. To see this, note that if the buyer furnishes a letter offering $d +$ "$lowc$", the seller will want to trade. Moreover, the buyer knows that the seller will want to deliver the letter to the third party/court. Since p is equal to "low c," the buyer extracts all of the surplus, which is equivalent to saying that they have all of the bargaining power.

Second, suppose that it is between "low c" and "high c." As before, the buyer can extract all of the surplus from renegotiation by furnishing a letter agreeing to a higher price if there is no trade.

---

[46] We follow Bolton and Dewatripont (2005: ch. 12) closely here.

Third, suppose that p is greater than "high c." Now the seller always wants to trade. Again, the buyer can extract all of the surplus from renegotiation by sending furnishing a letter agreeing to a higher price if there is no trade.

Taken together, this means that the buyer has all of the bargaining power and therefore has appropriate incentives to make the optimal level of investment.

Appendix B
Moore–Repullo Revelation Mechanism

Moore and Repullo (1988: 1208, 1212) present a multistage mechanism that permits implementation of any social objective, including truth telling, as the unique (subgame–perfect) equilibrium of the game induced by that mechanism. The following, based heavily on Aghion and Holden (2011) (see also Moore and Repullo 1988: 1196), is an example of this kind of mechanism in the context of the Apple–Corning example that we have been using.

(1) A(pple) announces either 40 or 32. If the announcement is 40, then A pays C(orning) a price equal to 40 and the mechanism stops.
(2) If A announces 32 and C does not challenge A's announcement, then A pays a price of 32 and the mechanism stops.
(3) If C challenges A's announcement, then
    (a) A pays a fine of 30 to a T(hird party)
    (b) A is offered the glass for 22
    (c) C gets 30 from T (and 22 from A for the glass), if A accepts
    (d) C pays 30 to T, if A rejects the glass
    (e) A and C Nash bargain over the glass.

We will not go through how to establish that truth telling is the unique equilibrium here, but we refer the interested reader to Aghion and Holden (2011: 191) for the requisite logic, although with different numerical values.

References

Aghion, Philippe, and Richard Holden. (2011) "Incomplete Contracts and the Theory of the Firm: What Have We Learned over the Past 25 Years?," *Journal of Economic Perspectives* 25: 181–197.

Aghion, Philippe, Mathias Dewatripont and Patrick Rey. (1994) "Renegotiation Design with Unverifiable Information," *Econometrica* 62: 257–282.

Aghion, Philippe, Drew Fudenberg, Richard Holden, Takashi Kunimoto and Olivier Tercieux (2012) "Subgame-Perfect Implementation under Information Perturbations," *Quarterly Journal of Economics* 127: 1843–1881.

Aghion, Philippe, Ernst Fehr, Richard Holden, and Tom Wilkening (2017) "The Role of Bounded Rationality and Imperfect Information in Subgame Perfect Implementation – An Empirical Investigation," *Journal of the European Economic Association* 16: 232–274.

Alaska Packers' Ass'n v. *Domenico*, 117 F. 99 (9th Cir. 1902).

Allison, Ian. (Apr. 30, 2016) "Ethereum Reinvents Companies with Launch of the DAO," available at www.ibtimes.co.uk/ethereum-reinvents-companies-launch-dao-1557576.

Altcointoday.com. (Apr. 22, 2017) "Bitcoin and Ethereum vs Visa and PayPal – Transactions per Second," available at www.altcointoday.com/bitcoin-ether eum-vs-visa-paypal-transactions-per-second/.

Althauser, Joshua. (Aug. 18, 2017) "Australian Government Moves to Regulate Cryptocurrency Exchanges," *Cointelegraph*, available at https://cointelegraph .com/news/australian-government-moves-to-regulate-cryptocurrency-exchanges.

Angel v. *Murray*, 322 A.2d 630 (R. I. 1974).

Antonopolous, Andreas M. (2nd ed., 2017) *Mastering Bitcoin: Programming the Open Blockchain*, O'Reilly Media.

Antràs, Pol. (2003) "Firms, Contracts, and Trade Structure," *Quarterly Journal of Economics* 118: 1375–1418.

Arruñada, Benito, and Luis Garicano. (2018) "Blockchain: The Birth of Decentralized Governance" Working Paper, available at https://ssrn.com/ abstract=3160070 or http://dx.doi.org/10.2139/ssrn.3160070.

Aru, Ikye. (Apr. 18, 2017) "Blockchain Transaction Anonymity Is Necessary Evil," *Cointelegraph*, available at https://cointelegraph.com/news/block chain-transaction-anonymity-is-necessary-evil.

Baker, George P., and Thomas N. Hubbard. (2004) "Contractibility and Asset Ownership: On-board Computers and Governance in U. S. Trucking," *Quarterly Journal of Economics* 119: 1443–1479.

Baker, Scott, and Anup Malani. (2014) "Trial Court Budgets, the Enforcer's Dilemma, and the Rule of Law," *University of Illinois Law Review* 2014: 1573–1602.

Bakos, Yannis, and Halaburda, Hanna. (May 26, 2019) "Smart Contracts, IoT Sensors and Efficiency: Automated Execution vs. Better Information" NYU Stern School of Business, available at https://ssrn.com/abstract=3394546 or http://dx.doi.org/10.2139/ssrn.3394546.

Baliga, Arati. (Apr.2017) "Understanding Blockchain Consensus Models" White Paper, available at www.persistent.com/wp-content/uploads/2017/04/WP-Understanding-Blockchain-Consensus-Models.pdf?pdf=Understanding-Blockchain-Consensus-Models.

Bar Gill, Oren, and Omri Ben Shahar. (2004) "The Law of Duress and the Economics of Credible Threats," *Journal of Legal Studies* 33: 391–430.

Beatty v. *Guggenheim Exploration Co.*, 122 N.E. 378, 387 (N.Y. 1919).

Bitcoin.org. (2021) "Bitcoin Developers Guide," available at https://bitcoin.org/en/developer-guide#block-chain.

Bitinfocharts.com. (2021a) "Bitcoin, Ethereum Transactions Historical Chart," available at https://bitinfocharts.com/comparison/transactions-btc-eth.html#3m.

Bitinfocharts.com. (2021b) "Bitcoin, Ethereum, Litecoin, Dogecoin Transactions Historical Chart," available at https://bitinfocharts.com/comparison/transactions-btc-eth-ltc-doge.html.

Blockgeeks.com. (2021a) "What Is Blockchain Technology? A Step-by-Step Guide for Beginners: An In-depth Guide by BlockGeeks," available at https://blockgeeks.com/guides/what-is-blockchain-technology/.

Blockgeeks.com. (2021b) "A Beginner's Guide to Smart Contracts," available at https://blockgeeks.com/guides/smart-contracts/.

Bolton, Patrick, and Mathias Dewatripont. (2005) *Contract Theory*, MIT.

Budish, Eric. (2018) "The Economic Limits of Bitcoin and the Blockchain" Working Paper, available at http://dx.doi.org/10.3386/w24717.

Buterin, Vitalik. (2014) "A Next Generation Smart Contract & Decentralized Application Platform: Ethereum Whitepaper," available at www.the-blockchain.com/docs/Ethereum_white_paper-a_next_generation_smart_contract_and_decentralized_application_platform-vitalik-buterin.pdf.

Buterin, Vitalik. (Dec. 30, 2016) "A Proof of Stake Design Philosophy," *Medium*, available at https://medium.com/@VitalikButerin/a-proof-of-stake-design-philosophy-506585978d51.

Calamari, John, and Joseph Perillo. (1983) *Contracts*, Hornbook.

Castor, Amy. (Mar. 14, 2017) "A (Short) Guide to Blockchain Consensus Protocols," *Coindesk*, available at www.coindesk.com/short-guide-block chain-consensus-protocols/.

Chirelstein, Marvin A. (3rd ed. 1998) *Concepts and Case Analysis in the Law of Contracts*, Foundation Press.

Christidis, Konstantinos, and Michael Devetsikiotis. (2016) "Blockchains and Smart Contracts for the Internet of Things," *IEEE Access* 4: 2292–2303.

Chung, Tai-Yeong. (1991) "Incomplete Contracts, Specific Investments, and Risk Sharing," *The Review of Economic Studies* 58: 1031–1042.

Coase, Ronald H. (1937) "The Nature of the Firm," *Economica* 4: 386–405.

Corbin, Arthur (1963) *Corbin on Contracts*, West Publishing.

Crook, Jordan. (Jul. 6, 2017) "This Apple Patent Application Could Describe Facial Recognition for the Next iPhone," *Techcrunch*, available at https:// techcrunch.com/2017/07/06/this-apple-patent-could-describe-facial-recogni tion-for-the-next-iphone/.

Crossman, Penny. (May 23, 2017) "Banks pour $107M into blockchain consortium R3, American Banker," *American Banker*, available at www .americanbanker.com/news/banks-pour-107m-into-blockchain-consor tium-r3.

Davis v. *Payne & Day, Inc.*, 348 P.2d 337, 339 (Utah 1960).

Dawson, Suzanne S., Robert J. Pence and David S. Stone (1987) "Poison Pill Defensive Measures," *Business Lawyer* 42: 423.

de Geest, Gerrit, and Filip Wuyts. (2000) "Penalty Clauses" in Gerrit de Geest (ed.), *Encyclopedia of Law and Economics Vol. 3: The Regulation of Contracts*, Edward Elgar, 141.

Domenico v. *Alaska Packers' Ass'n*, 112 F. 554 (N. D. Cal. 1901).

Easterbrook, Frank H. (1987) "Comparative Advantage and Antitrust Law," *California Law Review* 75: 983–990.

Easterbrook, Frank H. (1996) "Cyberspace and the Law of the Horse," *University of Chicago Legal Forum* 1996: 207.

Farnsworth, Edward Allan. (2003) *Farnsworth on Contracts*, Aspen Publishers.

Gibbons, Robert. (1992) *Game Theory for Applied Economists*, Princeton University Press.

Goldberg, Victor P. (1976) "Regulation and Administered Contracts," *Bell Journal of Economics and Management Science* 7: 426–448.

Graham, Daniel A., and Ellen R. Pierce. (1989) "Contract Modification: An Economic Analysis of the Hold-up Game," *Law and Contemporary Problems* 52: 9–32.

Gruson, Michael. (1980) "Governing Law Clauses in Commercial Agreements – New York's Approach," *Columbia Journal of Transnational Law* 18: 323–379.

Guerriero, Carmine. (Aug. 29, 2020) "Property Rights, Transaction Costs, and the Limits of the Market" Quaderni – Working Paper DSE N°1110, available at https://ssrn.com/abstract=3058095 or http://dx.doi.org/10.2139/ssrn.3058095.

Guerriero, Carmine, and Pignataro, Giuseppe. (Jan. 19, 2021) "Endogenous Property Rights and the Nature of the Firm" Working Paper, available at https://ssrn.com/abstract=3547522 or http://dx.doi.org/10.2139/ssrn.3547522.

Hart, Oliver, and John Moore. (1988) "Incomplete Contracts and Renegotiation," *Econometrica* 56: 755–785.

Hart, Oliver, and John Moore. (1990) "Property Rights and the Nature of the Firm," *Journal of Political Economy* 98: 1119–1158.

Hart, Oliver, and John Moore. (2008) "Contracts as Reference Points," *The Quarterly Journal of Economics* 123: 1–48.

Hartsville Oil Mill v. *United States*, 271 U.S. 43 (1926).

Holden, Richard, and Anup Malani. (2014) "Renegotiation Design by Contract," *University of Chicago Law Review* 81: 151–178.

Holmstrom, Bengt. (1982) "Moral Hazard in Teams," *Bell Journal of Economics* 13: 324–340.

Iansiti, Marco, and Karim R. Lakhani. (2017) "The Truth About Blockchain," *Harvard Business Review* 95: 118–127.

IRS. (2021) "List of Approved KYC Rules," available at www.irs.gov/businesses/international-businesses/list-of-approved-kyc-rules.

Jolls, Christine. (1997) "Contracts as Bilateral Commitments: A New Perspective on Contract Modification," *Journal of Legal Studies* 26: 203–237.

Kharpal, Arjun. (Aug. 9, 2017) "Initial Coin Offerings Have Raised $1.2 Billion and Now Surpass Early Stage VC Funding," *CNBC*, available at www.cnbc.com/2017/08/09/initial-coin-offerings-surpass-early-stage-venture-capital-funding.html.

Klein, Benjamin, Robert G. Crawford and Armen A. Alchian (1978) "Vertical Integration, Appropriable Rents, and the Competitive Contracting Process," *Journal of Law and Economics* 21: 297–326.

Laurence, Tiana. (2017) "Blockchain for Dummies," For Dummies.

Lee, Timothy B. (Sep. 15, 2017) "It Looks Like China Is Shutting Down Its Blockchain Economy," *Arstechnica*, available at https://arstechnica.com/tech-policy/2017/09/china-may-be-getting-ready-to-ban-bitcoin/.

López-Bayón, Susana, and Manuel González-Díaz. (2010) "Indefinite Contract Duration: Evidence from Electronics Subcontracting," *International Review of Law and Economics* 30: 145–159.

Marino, Bill. (Dec. 2, 2015) "Smart Contracts: The Next Big Blockchain Application," available at https://tech.cornell.edu/news/smart-contracts-the-next-big-blockchain-application.

Maskin, Eric. (1977) "Nash Equilibrium and Welfare Optimality" mimeo, ultimately published as Eric Maskin. (1999) "Nash Equilibrium and Welfare Optimality," *Review of Economic Studies* 66: 23–38.

Matonis, Jon. (Jan. 28, 2013) "Government Ban on Bitcoin Would Fail Miserably," *Forbes*, available at www.forbes.com/sites/jonmatonis/2013/01/28/government-ban-on-bitcoin-would-fail-miserably/#5d5e61c61d25.

Moore, John, and Rafael Repullo. (1988) "Subgame Perfect Implementation," *Econometrica* 56: 1191–1220.

John Edward Murray, Jr. (1974) *Contracts*, Hornbrook.

Nakamoto, Satoshi. (2008) "Bitcoin: A Peer-to-Peer Electronic Cash System" White Paper, available at www.ussc.gov/sites/default/files/pdf/training/annual-national-training-seminar/2018/Emerging_Tech_Bitcoin_Crypto.pdf.

Noldeke, Georg, and Klaus M. Schmidt. (1995) "Option Contracts and Renegotiation: A Solution to the Hold-up Problem," *RAND Journal of Economics* 26: 163–179.

Polinsky, A. Mitchell, and Steven Shavell. (1998) "Punitive Damages: An Economic Analysis," *Harvard Law Review* 111: 869–962.

Posner, R. A. (1977). Gratuitous promises in economics and law. *The Journal of Legal Studies, 6*(2), 411–426.

PWC. (Jan. 2013) "Know Your Customer: Quick Reference Guide," available at www.pwc.com/gx/en/financial-services/assets/pwc-kyc-anti-money-laundering-guide-2013.pdf.

Restatement (Second) of Contracts (1979), the American Law Institute.

Rogerson, William P. (1984) "Efficient Reliance and Damage Measures for Breach of Contract," *RAND Journal of Economics* 15: 39–53.

Rose v. *Daniels*, 8 R.I. 381 (1866).

Saleh, Fahad. (2021) "Blockchain without Waste: Proof-of-Stake," *Review of Financial Studies* 34 : 1156–1190.

Selten, Reinhard (1975) "Reexamination of the Perfectness Concept for Equilibrium Points in Extensive Games," *International Journal of Game Theory* 4: 25–55.

Serafine, Mary Lou. (1991) "Note, Repudiated Compromise after Breach," *Yale Law Journal* 100: 2229.

Shavell, Steven. (2007) "Contractual Hold-up and Legal Intervention," *Journal of Legal Studies* 36: 325–354.

Siegfried, Nils, Tobias Rosenthal and Alexander Benlian. (Jan. 2020) "Blockchain and the Industrial Internet of Things," *Journal of Enterprise Information Management*, available at https://doi.org/10.1108/JEIM-06-2018-0140.

Sistrom v. *Anderson*, 51 Cal. App. 2d 213, 124 P.2d 372 (1942).

Stark, Josh. (Jun. 4, 2016) "Making Sense of Blockchain Smart Contracts," *Coindesk*, available at www.coindesk.com/making-sense-smart-contracts/.

Steinberg Press, Inc. v. *Charles Henry Publications, Inc.*, 68 N.Y.S.2d 793 (N.Y. Sup. Ct. 1947).

Szabo, Nick. (2021) "Smart Contracts: Building Blocks for Digital Market, Entropy #16," available at www.fon.hum.uva.nl/rob/Courses/InformationInSpeech/CDROM/Literature/LOTwinterschool2006/szabo.best.vwh.net/smart_contracts_2.html.

Tarver Robertson, Christopher. (2010) "Blind Expertise," *NYU Law Review* 85: 174–257.

Threedy, Debora L. (2000) "A Fish Story: *Alaska Packers' Association* v. *Domenico*," *Utah Law Review*: 185.

Tidmarsh, Jay. (Mar. 19, 2015) "Out of Court, Out of Luck," *US News & World Report*, available at www.usnews.com/opinion/economic-intelligence/2015/03/19/consumer-protection-bureau-arbitration-report-provides-much-needed-data.

Tinn, Katrin. (2017) "Blockchain and the Future of Optimal Financing Contracts" Working Paper, available at https://ssrn.com/abstract=3061532 or http://dx.doi.org/10.2139/ssrn.3061532.

Torbert, Preston M. (2017) "A Study of the Risks of Contract Ambiguity," *PKU Transnational Law Review* 2: 1–114.

US Department of State. (Mar. 7, 2012) "Major Money Laundering Countries," available at www.state.gov/j/inl/rls/nrcrpt/2012/vol2/184112.htm.

White, James, and Robert Summers. (3rd ed. 1988) *Uniform Commercial Code*, Hornbrook.

Wikipedia. (2021a) "Satoshi Nakamoto," available at https://en.wikipedia.org/wiki/Satoshi_Nakamoto.

Wikipedia. (2021b) "Sandbox (Software Development)," available at https://en.wikipedia.org/wiki/Sandbox_(software_development).

Williamson, Oliver. (1975) *Markets and Hierarchies: Analysis and Antitrust Implications*, Free Press.

Williamson, Oliver E. (1979) "Transaction-Cost Economics: The Governance of Contractual Relations," *Journal of Law and Economics* 22: 233–261.

Zheng, Zibin, Shaoan Xie, Hongning Dai, Xiangping Chen and Huaimin Wang. (2018) "Blockchain Challenges and Opportunities: A Survey," *International Journal of Web and Grid Services* 14: 352–375.

Zumwinkel v. *Leggett*, 345 S.W.2d 89, 93–94 (Mo. 1961).

Acknowledgments

We thank the editors, four anonymous referees, Ilya Beylin, Anthony Casey, Stacy Rosenbaum, Pat Ward, and Massimo Young for comments.

Cambridge Elements ☰

Law, Economics and Politics

Series Editor in Chief
Carmine Guerriero, *University of Bologna*

Series Co-Editors
Rosa Ferrer, *UPF and Barcelona GSE*
Nuno Garoupa, *George Mason University*
Mariana Mota Prado, *University of Toronto*
Murat Mungan, *George Mason University*

Series Managing Editor
Liam Wells, *Erasmus University, Rotterdam*

Series Associate Editors
Tim Friehe, *Philipps-Universität Marburg*
Marie Obidzinski, *Université Paris 2*
Anna Bindler, *University of Cologne*
Jo Seldeslachts, *University of Amsterdam*
Andy Hanssen, *Clemson University*
Sara Biancini, *Université de Cergy-Pontoise*
Pedro Magalhães, *ICS, Lisbon*
Kelly Rader, *Yale University*
Jed Kroncke, *Hong Kong University*
Sara Ghebremusse, *University of British Columbia*

About the Series
Individual decision-making is influenced by formal rules (including laws), legal and political 'institutions', and 'informal institutions' influenced by social norms. These institutions determine the nature, scope and operation of markets, organisations and states. This interdisciplinary series analyses the functioning, determinants and impact of these institutions, organizing the existing knowledge and guiding future research.

Law, Economics and Politics

Elements in the Series

Printed in the United States
by Baker & Taylor Publisher Services